KS2 Success

LEARN AND PRACTISE

Maths and English

Paul Broadbent and Lynn Huggins-Cooper

Contents

Using and applying mathematics

Problem-solving 6
Money 8
Number sequences 10

Counting and understanding numbers

Three-digit numbers 12
Comparing and ordering 14
Rounding numbers 16
Fractions 18

Knowing and using number facts

Addition and subtraction facts 20
Multiplication facts 22

Calculating

Mental addition 24
Mental subtraction 26
Written addition and subtraction 28
Division 30

Understanding shape

2D shapes	32
3D shapes	34
Reflective symmetry	36
Directions and angles	38

Measuring

Measurement	40
Reading the time	42

Handling data

Graphs and charts	44

Test Practice

Test practice	46

Glossary

Glossary	52

Contents

Speaking and listening

Speaking and listening 54

Word structure and spelling

Prefixes 56
Homonyms and homophones 58
Contractions 60
Suffixes 62
Spelling strategy 1 64
Spelling strategy 2 66

Sentence structure and punctuation

Verbs 68
Adjectives 70
Pronouns 72
Speech marks 74
Questions and exclamations 76

Understanding text

Understanding text 78

Creating and shaping texts

Synonyms for said 80
Active and passive verbs 82
Reports and conjunctions 84
Recounts 86
Writing stories 88
Letters 90

Text structure and organisation

Shape poems 92

Test practice

Spelling 94
Handwriting 95
Story writing 96
Comprehension 98
Writing letters 100

Glossary

Glossary 101

Maths and English Answers

Answer pages (detachable from the back of the book) 1–8

Problem-solving

Read word problems carefully to work out the calculations that are needed. Always follow these four easy steps:

Step 1: Read the problem.
Try to picture the problem and imagine going through it in real life.

Step 2: Sort out the calculations.
You might need to add, subtract, multiply or divide. Sometimes more than one calculation is needed.

Step 3: Answer the calculations.
Work out the answers carefully.

Step 4: Answer the problem.
Look back at the question – what is it asking?

Exercise 1

Answer these problems.

a A candle is 26cm long. It burns down 18cm.
   How long is it now? _____

b Josh has 90 stamps in his collection and is given another
   10 by his aunt. How many stamps are there altogether? _____

c Eve had 12 friends and 7 relatives at her party.
   How many people did Eve invite to her party in total? _____

d Mrs French has 70p and spends 25p on a newspaper.
   How much money has she got left? _____

e Kate is 10, her mother is 40 and her gran is 70.
   What is their total age? _____

f How old was Gran when Kate was born? _____

Exercise 2

Answer these.

a At the school cake stall Mr Green buys 5 biscuits at 9p each and 2 cakes that cost 30p each. What is the total cost of Mr Green's biscuits and cakes? _____

b There are 6 eggs in a box. 5 full egg boxes have been dropped and 8 eggs are broken. How many eggs are left? _____

c Gina collected 25 conkers, Ali collected 20 and Matt collected 15. They put all the conkers together and shared them equally. How many conkers did they each get? _____

d Mrs Khan bought a book for £4, a pen for £3 and a CD for £12. How much change did she get from £20? _____

e These are the ingredients to make 10 currant buns. 120g flour, 40g sugar, 30g butter, 60g egg, 50g currants. How much will each bun weigh? _____

Challenge

Make up your own maths problem, by writing down any calculation, such as 12 + 6 = 18. Then make up a word problem for this calculation.

For example: An elephant stored 12 nuts at the top of a tree and 6 more at the bottom. How many nuts did he store altogether?

Try this for different calculations.

Brain Teaser

Try these 'think of a number' problems:

1 I think of a number, then add 5.
   The answer is 13. What was my number?

2 I think of a number, then subtract 11.
   The answer is 17. What was my number?

3 I think of a number, then multiply by 3.
   The answer is 21. What was my number?

USING AND APPLYING MATHEMATICS

Money

These are the coins and notes that we use.

There are 100 pence in £1. We use a **decimal point** to show the pounds and the pence: £1.85.

£2.50 = 250p £5.00 = 500p £3.25 = 325p

Exercise 1

Total each amount.

a

b

c

d

£ ☐   ☐ p   £ ☐   ☐ p

Exercise 2

What is the change from £2 for each of these?

a £1.30 ☐   b 90p ☐   c £1.05 ☐

d £1.75 ☐   e 40p ☐   f 75p ☐

8

Exercise 3

Look at the picture and then answer the questions.

a How much would two bags of food cost?

b What is the total cost of a cage, water bottle and exercise wheel?

c How much change would you get from £5 if you bought the exercise ball?

d How much more is the wheel than the exercise ball?

e Harry has 4 coins. It is exactly enough money to buy a bag of food. What are the four coins Harry has? Draw them in this wallet.

Top Tip

To work out an amount of change, count on from the cost of the item to the amount given.

If something costs £1.65, the change from £2 is 35p.

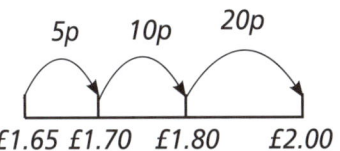

Challenge

Grab a shopping catalogue and see if you can use it to reach target amounts. For example, give yourself a target of £20 to spend. Choose a page and try to estimate spending just under £20 on different numbers of items. Check your estimate with a calculator. If you go over £20 you lose – if you are close to £20 you win. The target can be changed to £50. Why don't you have a go?

Brain Teaser

Use five coins to make these different amounts.

1 £1.36

2 £2.67

3 94p

4 £3.13

Number sequences

Number **sequences** are patterns of numbers with the same-sized steps.

Sequences can go up:

3 5 7 9 …

40 50 60 70 …

or down:

900 800 700 600 …

34 32 30 28 …

To work out missing numbers in sequences, look at the **difference** between each number.

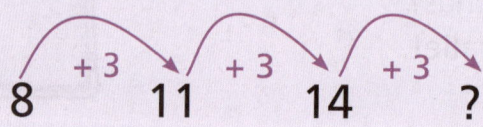

The next number is 17.

Exercise 1

Write the next three numbers in each of these sequences.

a 27   29   31   33

b 80   78   76   74

c 42   52   62   72

d 112 212 312 412

e 96   86   76   66

f 168 158 148 138

Exercise 2

Write the missing numbers in each of these sequences.

a 9   13   17   ☐   ☐   29   ☐   37

b 31   28   ☐   22   19   16   ☐   ☐

c 6   11   ☐   21   26   ☐   ☐   41

d 54   ☐   46   42   38   ☐   ☐   26

Exercise 3

Circle the even numbers in these number lines.

a 137   138   139   140   141   142

b 240   239   238   237   236   235

c 809   810   811   812   813   814   815   816

Top Tip: Odd numbers end in 1, 3, 5, 7 and 9.
Even numbers end in 0, 2, 4, 6 and 8.

Challenge

A fun way to learn about number sequences is to look at car registration plates and try to spot any three numbers that show a sequence.

For example: T147 RFW has a +3 sequence: 1 (+3) 4 (+3) 7

Next time you're in the car, why don't you have a go?

Brain Teaser

Number sequences can include negative numbers. Write the missing numbers on these number lines.

1 ☐   ☐   −2   −1   0   1   ☐

2 −3   ☐   ☐   ☐   1   2   ☐

USING AND APPLYING MATHEMATICS

Three-digit numbers

Numbers are made from the ten **digits**:

0 1 2 3 4 5 6 7 8 9

The important thing to remember is that the position of a digit in a number gives its value.

458 = 400 + 50 + 8

hundreds   tens   ones

To multiply by 10 move all the digits one place to the left.

The empty place is filled by a zero.

38 × 10 =
380

To divide by 10 move all the digits one place to the right.

490 ÷ 10 =
49

Exercise 1

Join the numbers to the words.

six hundred and ninety-four

three hundred and sixty-eight

one hundred and twenty-four

368

964

124

680

683

694

six hundred and eighty

nine hundred and sixty-four

six hundred and eighty-three

Exercise 2

Write the missing numbers.

a 495 = 400 + ☐ + 5

b 538 = ☐ + ☐ + ☐

c 746 = ☐ + ☐ + ☐

d 734 = ☐ + ☐ + ☐

e 849 = ☐ + ☐ + ☐

f 293 = ☐ + ☐ + ☐

Exercise 3

Write the numbers coming out of each machine.

a 68      b 320

42   400

81   740

90   680

Top Tip: Zero is a very important digit. It is easy to confuse the numbers 204, 240, 2040 and 2400. For numbers like these, look carefully at the position of the zeros.

Challenge

Playing Digit Boxes is fun on your own or with a friend. Use digit cards 0-9 shuffled and placed face down.

Draw three boxes and then turn over the top card. Write the digit in one of the boxes, with the aim to make the largest 3-digit number possible.

Once the digit is written, repeat this twice more until the 3-digit number is complete. Is it the largest number possible? Try it with 4-digit numbers.

Brain Teaser

Which number is each arrow pointing to?

1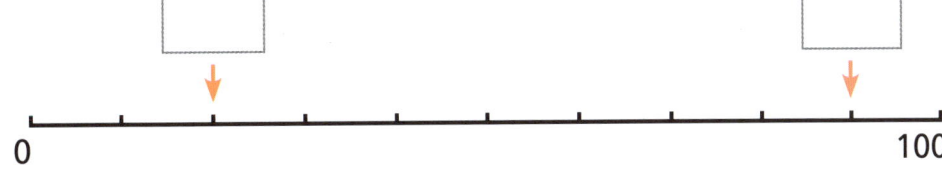

2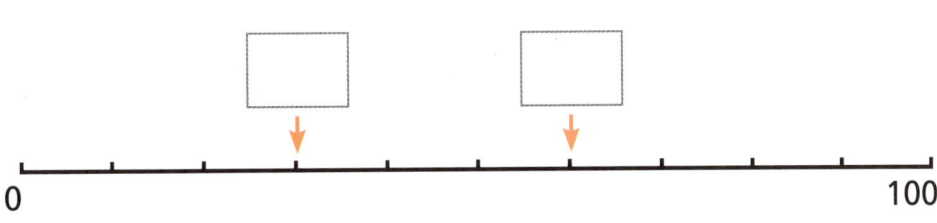

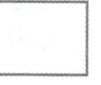

Comparing and ordering

When you need to **compare** numbers to find the largest or smallest, it is helpful to write them under each other, lining up the units.

For example: Josh scored 748 points on a computer game, and Emma scored 780. Who got the highest score?

Line them up:

hundreds	tens	ones
7	4	8
7	8	0

Compare the hundreds, tens and ones and you can see that 780 is bigger because it has 8 tens.

You can use the same method to put a set of numbers in order of size.

Put these in order starting with the smallest:

154   290   406   298

Line them up and put them in order:

hundreds	tens	ones
1	5	4
2	9	0
2	9	8
4	0	6

Exercise 1

Circle the smallest number in each pair.

a 412   242   b 606   660   c 594   592   d 800   796

Exercise 2

Write a number on each card so that the five numbers are in size order.

a 384   ☐   399   ☐   406

b ☐   615   ☐   637   648

c 825   ☐   ☐   878   891

Exercise 3

Write these amounts in order, starting with the smallest.

a 714ml   284ml   738ml   480ml   842ml

_____ _____ _____ _____ _____

b 856g   865g   560g   681g   650g

_____ _____ _____ _____ _____

Exercise 4

Join these numbers to their correct positions.

381   337   314   373   356

300 ——————————————————————————— 400

 **Top Tip** Remember to read each number from the left to the right. Compare all the hundreds first and put them in order, then the tens, and finally the ones.

Challenge

Use digit cards 0–9. Pick out any four cards and make as many different 3-digit numbers as you can. Write them in order, starting with the smallest.

How many different 3-digit numbers can you make? How many 2-digit or 4-digit numbers can you make? Try it with different sets of digits.

Brain Teaser

Each of these should be in order. Colour the two numbers that have been swapped in each row.

1 214 215 219 217 218 216

2 375 370 373 372 371 374

3 684 682 683 681 685 686

Rounding numbers

Rounding makes numbers easier to work with – changing them to the nearest ten or hundred.

Rounding to the nearest 10.
- Look at the ones digit.
- If it is 5 or more, round up the tens digit.
- If it is less than 5, the tens digit stays the same.

35 rounds up to 40.

64 rounds down to 60.

30   35   40   60   64   70

Rounding to the nearest 100.
- Look at the tens digits.
- If it is 50 or more, round up the hundreds digit.
- If it is less than 50, the hundreds digit stays the same.

763 rounds up to 800.

537 rounds down to 500.

700   763   800   500   537   600

Exercise 1

Round these numbers to the nearest 10.

a 48 → ☐   d 83 → ☐   g 59 → ☐

b 75 → ☐   e 56 → ☐   h 64 → ☐

c 12 → ☐   f 47 → ☐   i 35 → ☐

Exercise 2

Round these numbers to the nearest 100.

a 317 → ☐   d 264 → ☐   g 548 → ☐

b 184 → ☐   e 706 → ☐   h 850 → ☐

c 210 → ☐   f 638 → ☐   i 192 → ☐

Exercise 3

Join these numbers to the nearest 10.

27 42 58 74 85 96

10   20   30   40   50   60   70   80   90   100

Exercise 4

Write five numbers that you would round to 400 (to the nearest 100).

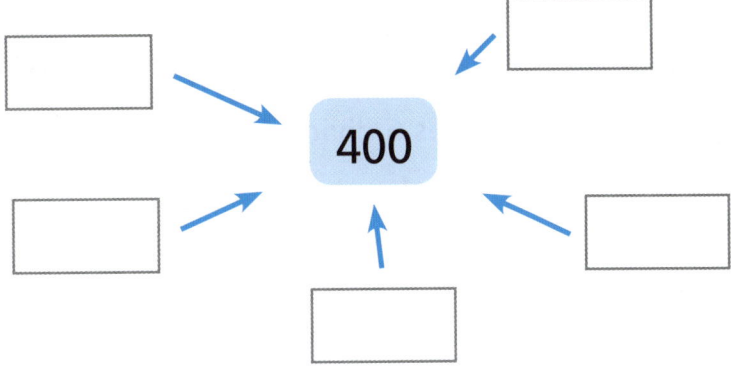

 **Top Tip** We round up if the number is halfway between two tens or two hundreds. So, for example, 35 rounds up to 40 and 250 rounds up to 300.

Challenge

Choose a big book with lots of pages. Make sure you can lift it! Open it up at any page and look at the page number. Work out which number this rounds to, to the nearest 10, and then check by counting on or back through the pages. This is a good way of checking how quick and accurate you are at rounding.

Brain Teaser

Each of these needs rounding to the nearest 100. Circle the correct answer.

1 1428 → 1500   1430   1400
2 3084 → 3000   3100   3090
3 6245 → 6200   6250   6300

Fractions

When you read or write a **fraction**, the bottom part of the fraction, or **denominator**, tells you the number of equal parts.

Look at these:

 → $\frac{1}{2}$ → one half → one whole divided into 2 equal parts

 → $\frac{1}{4}$ → one quarter → one whole divided into 4 equal parts

 → $\frac{1}{10}$ → one tenth → one whole divided into 10 equal parts

To find fractions of amounts, just divide by the denominator.

$\frac{1}{3}$ of 6 is the same as 6 divided by 3, which is 2

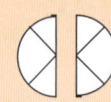

Exercise 1

Write the fraction that each shape is shaded.

a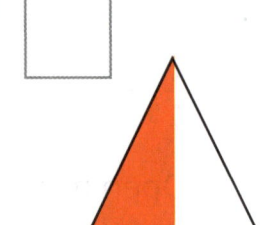

b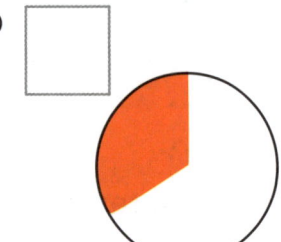

c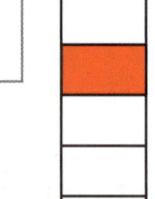

d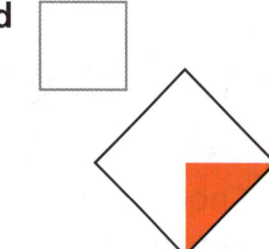

Exercise 2

Colour these shapes to show the fractions.

a $\frac{1}{4}$

b $\frac{1}{5}$

c $\frac{1}{2}$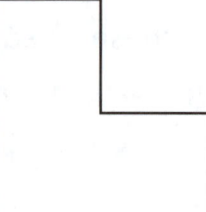

Exercise 3

Draw loops around the sweets to show the fraction. Write the answers.

a $\frac{1}{4}$ of 12 = ☐   b $\frac{1}{2}$ of 6 = ☐   c $\frac{1}{3}$ of 12 = ☐

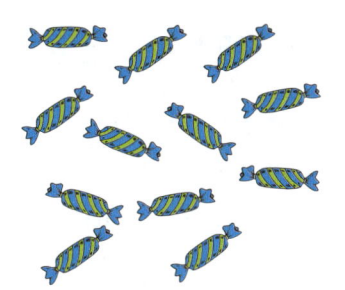

Exercise 4

Colour $\frac{1}{4}$ of this flag red. Colour $\frac{1}{2}$ blue.

Top Tip: *The same fraction can look different. All these are the same as a half.*

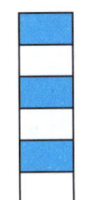
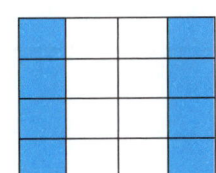
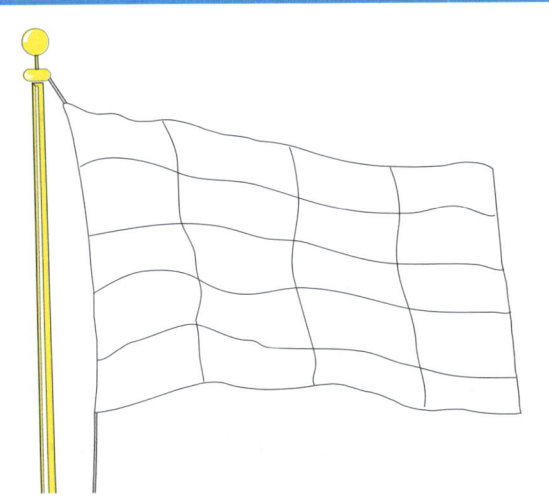

Challenge

You can make half patterns, just draw a square grid of 16 squares. Now shade half of the squares to make a colourful pattern. How many squares will be coloured?

Repeat this on other grids to make different half patterns.

Brain Teaser

What must be added to each of these fractions to make 1?

1 $\frac{1}{2}$ + ☐   2 $\frac{1}{4}$ + ☐

3 $\frac{2}{3}$ + ☐   4 $\frac{1}{10}$ + ☐

5 $\frac{7}{10}$ + ☐   6 $\frac{4}{9}$ + ☐

COUNTING AND UNDERSTANDING NUMBERS

Addition and subtraction facts

KNOWING AND USING NUMBER FACTS

When you add two numbers together, the order in which you add does not matter.

> 4 + 7 is the same as 7 + 4.

You can start with either number. This means that you have half as many addition facts to remember. If you know the answer to 8 + 4, then you also know the answer to 4 + 8.

When you subtract, the order does matter.

> 12 − 5 is not the same as 5 − 12.

It is important to know which number you are starting with, so you can then take an amount away from it.

> Make sure you know these three signs:
> **+** is the addition sign   **−** is the subtraction sign
> **=** is the equal sign

Exercise 1

Complete these addition squares.

a

+	4	6	2
7	11		
3			
8			

b

+	6	3	11
5	11		
9			
4			

c

+	6	4	5
12	18		
14			
9			

Exercise 2

Write the difference between each pair of numbers.

a 14   9 ☐

b 8   11 ☐

c 17   14 ☐

d 6   13 ☐

e 15   8 ☐

f 19   13 ☐

Exercise 3

Try to answer each column of sums as quickly as you can.
Time yourself to find your quickest time.

a 7 + 2 = ☐   b 7 + 6 = ☐   c 5 − 2 = ☐   d 18 − 9 = ☐

   5 + 3 = ☐   8 + 7 = ☐   8 − 6 = ☐   11 − 3 = ☐

   2 + 8 = ☐   6 + 5 = ☐   6 − 1 = ☐   14 − 6 = ☐

   4 + 6 = ☐   4 + 9 = ☐   10 − 3 = ☐   12 − 6 = ☐

   3 + 4 = ☐   5 + 8 = ☐   8 − 4 = ☐   17 − 8 = ☐

   2 + 5 = ☐   4 + 7 = ☐   7 − 3 = ☐   16 − 9 = ☐

   6 + 3 = ☐   8 + 8 = ☐   10 − 5 = ☐   12 − 8 = ☐

   4 + 5 = ☐   9 + 6 = ☐   9 − 8 = ☐   11 − 2 = ☐

Top Tip Use addition facts that you know to help work out subtraction facts.
For example, if you know that 7 + 5 = 12, then you can use this to work out 12 − 5 or 12 − 7.

Challenge

Let's play Tennis Sums!

Find a friend, then start by 'serving' to your friend with an addition or subtraction fact. They work out the answer quickly and return a fact back using the answer as the first number. You continue backwards and forwards until someone makes a mistake. The answers must not be above 20.

So a game could be like this:

   8 add 4 is ?   12 take away 3 is ?
   9 take away 6 is ?   3 add 12 is ?
            15… and so on.
                Have fun!

Brain Teaser

Write + or − in each circle to make these true.

1   7 ◯ 4 ◯ 3 = 14

2   9 ◯ 2 ◯ 8 = 15

3   6 ◯ 3 ◯ 4 = 5

4   8 ◯ 2 ◯ 4 = 2

5   11 ◯ 6 ◯ 3 = 14

KNOWING AND USING NUMBER FACTS

Multiplication facts

Use this grid to help you learn the multiplication facts for 2×, 3×, 4×, 5×, 6× and 10×.

×	0	1	2	3	4	5	6	7	8	9	10
2	0	2	4	6	8	10	12	14	16	18	20
3	0	3	6	9	12	15	18	21	24	27	30
4	0	4	8	12	16	20	24	28	32	36	40
5	0	5	10	15	20	25	30	35	40	45	50
6	0	6	12	18	24	30	36	42	48	54	60
10	0	10	20	30	40	50	60	70	80	90	100

You can multiply in any order.

4 × 3 has the same answer as 3 × 4.

They both equal 12.

Exercise 1

Complete the boxes in four different ways.

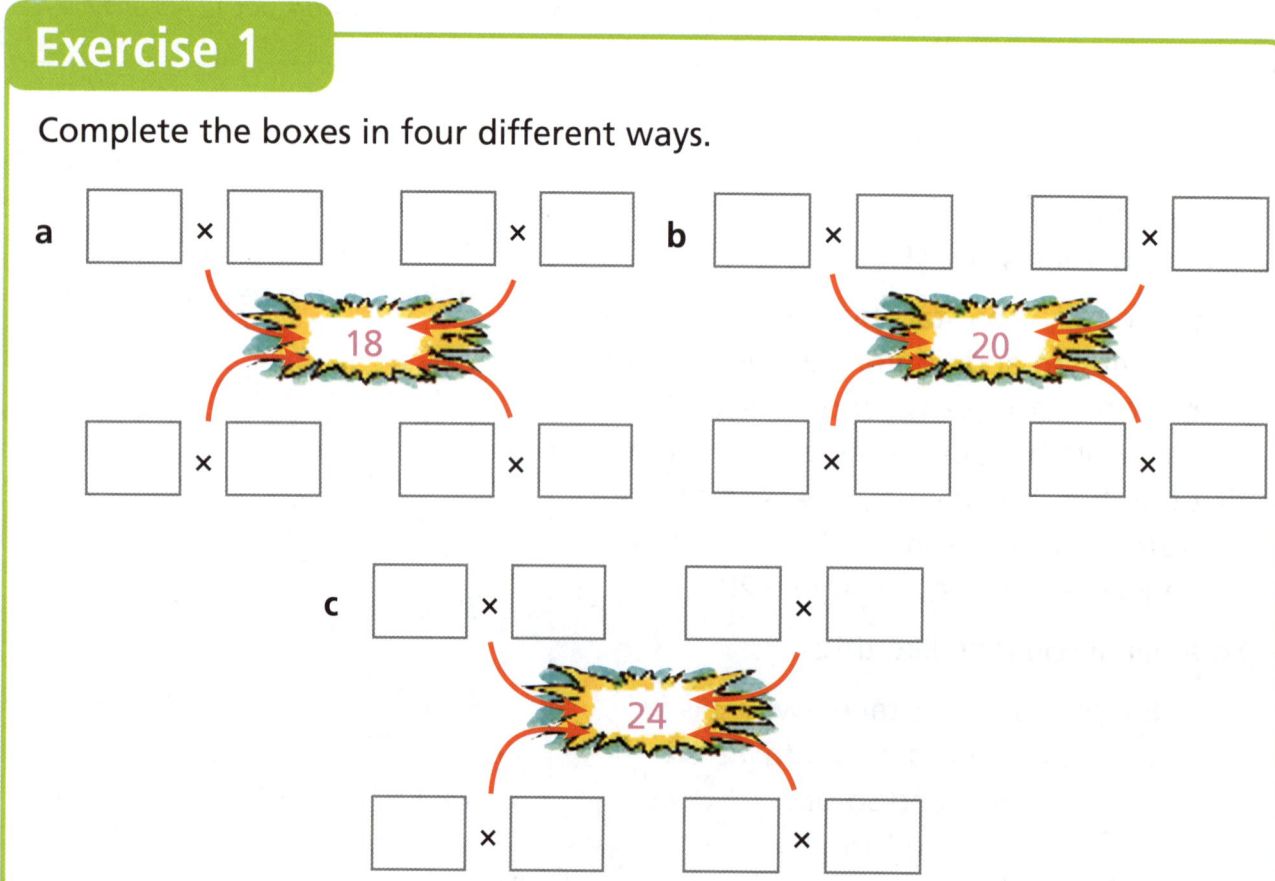

Exercise 2

Answer these as quickly as you can. Time yourself to find your quickest time.

a 7 × 2 = ☐   b 8 × 3 = ☐   c 7 × 9 = ☐

   4 × 4 = ☐   9 × 2 = ☐   5 × 8 = ☐

   5 × 9 = ☐   5 × 5 = ☐   6 × 3 = ☐

   3 × 8 = ☐   6 × 7 = ☐   4 × 7 = ☐

   6 × 6 = ☐   10 × 4 = ☐   9 × 8 = ☐

   4 × 3 = ☐   4 × 9 = ☐   5 × 6 = ☐

Exercise 3

Complete each table.

a IN → × 3 → OUT

IN	4		10		3
OUT		15		21	

b IN → × 4 → OUT

IN	2		7		5
OUT		32		16	

Top Tip: Use any facts you already know to help work out others quickly. For example:

If you know 5 × 3 = 15 then 6 × 3 is only 3 more → 18.
If you know that 4 × 4 = 16 then 8 × 4 is double 16 → 32.

Challenge

Try this challenge.

Make cards for each of the facts for the 2x, 3x, 4x, 5x and 10x tables. Write the answers on the back of each card. Shuffle them and lay them in a pile face up. Set a timer and see how many facts you can answer correctly in 30 seconds. Check each answer as you go along. Keep a record of the number you get right and then after a few days see if you can beat your best score.

|2 × 6| |4 × 4|

Brain Teaser

Draw on the path that each number should take across the maze.

Each number can only land on a multiplication that has itself as the answer.

40 → | 1×40 | 8×5 | 3×12 | 2×18 | → home

24 → | 2×12 | 4×9 | 2×20 | 4×10 | → home

36 → | 6×6 | 4×6 | 3×8 | 24×1 | → home

KNOWING AND USING NUMBER FACTS

23

Mental addition

CALCULATING

Once you know your addition facts, you can use them to help work out harder sums.

Adding tens:
4 + 5 = 9
40 + 50 = 90

Adding on small numbers:
7 + 4 = 11
37 + 4 = 41

Using near-doubles:
8 + 8 = 16
80 + 82 = 162

There are lots of different ways to add 2-digit numbers.
Try these methods for 46 + 38:

40 + 30 = 70
6 + 8 = 14
70 + 14 = 84

46 + 30 = 76
76 + 8 = 84

38 is 2 less than 40
46 + 40 = 86
86 − 2 = 84

Exercise 1

Answer these.

a 40 + 30 = ☐
   46 + 30 = ☐

b 50 + 60 = ☐
   53 + 62 = ☐

c 20 + 70 = ☐
   29 + 76 = ☐

d 40 + 80 = ☐
   40 + 84 = ☐

e 60 + 30 = ☐
   61 + 35 = ☐

f 80 + 50 = ☐
   87 + 57 = ☐

g 70 + 40 = ☐
   70 + 47 = ☐

h 30 + 80 = ☐
   30 + 81 = ☐

i 70 + 60 = ☐
   77 + 62 = ☐

Exercise 2

Add the rows and columns. Check the totals with the corner numbers.

a
19	24	
32	18	
		93

b
21	34	
26	17	
		98

c
15	31	
24	29	
		99

Exercise 3

Join pairs of numbers that total 100.

63   72   45   82   18

                35   27

73   37   65   28   55

Top Tip: Adding 19, 29, 39, 49 and so on, is easy because they are so close to a tens number.

34 + 29 is the same as
34 + 30 − 1 ➔ 64 − 1 = 63

Challenge

Look at this magic square.

All the rows, columns and diagonals add up to the same amount.

4	3	8
9	5	1
2	7	6

Try finishing this magic square. It uses the numbers 1 to 16.

1			4
12			
	11		
13		3	16

Have a go at making up your own magic squares.

Brain Teaser

Answer these questions using the five numbers below.

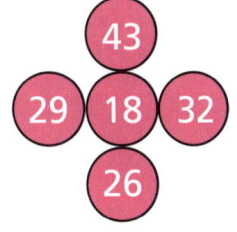

1 Which two numbers total 55? _____

2 What is the smallest total that can be made by adding two numbers? _____

3 What is the largest even total made by adding two numbers? _____

4 Which three numbers total 90? _____

Mental subtraction

There are lots of different ways to subtract 2-digit numbers. One of the best ways is to count on from the smaller number to the nearest ten.

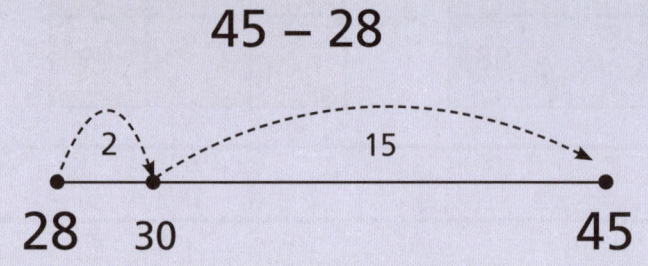

Count on from 28 to 30 and hold the 2 in your head.

30 on to 45 is 15.

15 add 2 is 17.

So the difference between 28 and 45 is 17

45 − 28 = 17.

Exercise 1

Use the number lines to help answer these. Count on to the nearest ten and draw the jumps.

a 36 − 17 = ☐

17 ———————————— 36

b 41 − 28 = ☐

28 ———————————— 41

c 44 − 19 = ☐

19 ———————————— 44

d 62 − 37 = ☐

37 ———————————— 62

e 53 − 26 = ☐

26 ———————————— 53

Exercise 2

Write the difference between these pairs of numbers.

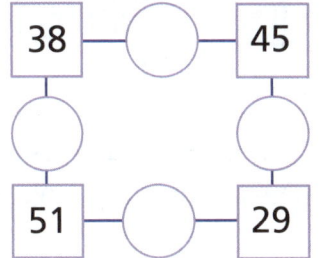
a

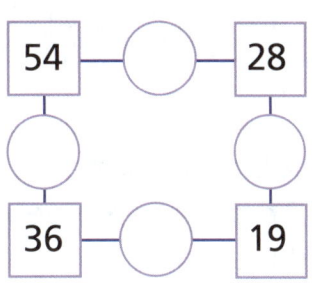
b

Top Tip: Taking away 19, 29, 39, 49, and so on, is easy because they are so close to a tens number.

54 − 29 is the same as 54 − 30 then add 1.

Exercise 3

Write the missing number in each sum.

a 34 − ☐ = 19

b 52 − 13 = ☐

c 65 − ☐ = 25

d ☐ − 36 = 24

e ☐ − 47 = 17

f 83 − ☐ = 56

g ☐ − 48 = 92

h 76 − ☐ = 28

Challenge

Here's a game to test how good your mental subtraction powers are.

Write down any 2-digit number, such as 62. Reverse the digits and write down that number ➔ 26.

Find the difference between the two numbers: 62 − 26 = 36

Add up the two digits from the answer: 3 + 6 = 9

Try doing the same thing with other digits and reverse subtractions. What do you notice?

Brain Teaser

Answer these questions using the five numbers.

a 41   b 27   c 32   d 19   e 25

1 Which two numbers have a difference of 7? ___ ___

2 What is a take away d? ___

3 Which number is 16 less than a? ___

4 a − c = d. True or false? ___

CALCULATING

Written addition and subtraction

Sometimes numbers for adding or taking away are just too big and tricky to work out in your head. That's when a pen and paper are handy! Look at these written methods and practise using the methods you prefer.

Addition:

78 + 64

```
   7 8              7 8
 + 6 4            + 6 4
   1 2  → 8 + 4    1 4 2
 1 3 0  → 70 + 60    1
 1 4 2
```

Subtraction:

94 − 67

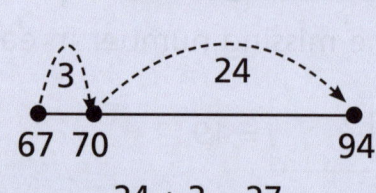

24 + 3 = 27

```
   8 1
   9 4      94 is broken
 − 6 7      up into 80
   2 7      and 14
```

Exercise 1

Answer these.

a) 58
  + 37

b) 123
  + 59

c) 56
  + 37

d) 275
  + 56

e) 94
  + 41

f) 138
  + 42

g) 95
  + 79

h) 486
  + 24

Exercise 2

Answer these.

a) 83
   − 57
   ____

b) 181
   − 76
   ____

c) 304
   − 62
   ____

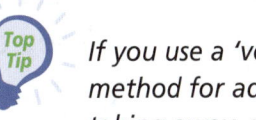

Top Tip: If you use a 'vertical' written method for adding or taking away, make sure you line up the columns carefully. Ones should be above ones, tens above tens and hundreds above hundreds. Written addition and subtraction is easier if you start with the ones column and work your way left.

d) 94
   − 39
   ____

e) 213
   − 81
   ____

f) 158
   − 90
   ____

Exercise 3

Answer these.

a) ☐ 7
   + 3 8
   _____
     9 ☐

b) ☐ 6 5
   + ☐ 9
   _____
     4 2 4

c) ☐ 3 ☐
   −   8 6
   _____
     4 4

d) 1 ☐ 4
   +   4 ☐
   _____
     2 0 7

e) 1 ☐ 7
   −   5 ☐
   _____
     1 4 4

Challenge

Compare your written method with your mental method for adding or taking away. Use a mental method and then a written method for 58 + 37 and 64 − 36. Which was quicker? Are they similar methods? Can you explain your methods to someone else? Try the same thing with larger numbers.

Brain Teaser

The digits 1 to 7 are missing. Write them in the correct places.

  1 8 ☐
+   4 7
_____
  ☐ 3 0

  2 1 6
−   5 ☐
_____
  ☐ ☐ 2

  2 9 ☐
+   ☐ 4
_____
  3 5 1

CALCULATING

Division

4, 5 and 20 are a **trio**. They can make different multiplication and division facts.

$$4 \times 5 = 20 \qquad 5 \times 4 = 20 \qquad 20 \div 5 = 4 \qquad 20 \div 4 = 5$$

This is useful for working out division facts.

$18 \div 3 = \boxed{}$ Change it to a multiplication fact.

$3 \times \boxed{} = 18$ The missing number is 6.

The division sign is ÷

Exercise 1

Answer these.

a How many twos in 12?

   $12 \div 2 = \boxed{}$

b How many fours in 20?

   $20 \div 4 = \boxed{}$

c How many tens in 70?

   $70 \div 10 = \boxed{}$

d How many fives in 15?

   $15 \div 5 = \boxed{}$

e How many threes in 18?

   $18 \div 3 = \boxed{}$

f How many fours in 12?

   $12 \div 4 = \boxed{}$

Exercise 2

Write the answers and remainders.

a $12 \div 5 = \boxed{}$ r $\boxed{}$

b $15 \div 2 = \boxed{}$ r $\boxed{}$

c $22 \div 3 = \boxed{}$ r $\boxed{}$

d $54 \div 10 = \boxed{}$ r $\boxed{}$

e $19 \div 4 = \boxed{}$ r $\boxed{}$

f $32 \div 3 = \boxed{}$ r $\boxed{}$

Exercise 3

Answer these problems. Check whether you need to round up or down.

a There are 28 children in a class. One table seats 5 children. How many tables are needed?

b A farmer collects 38 eggs. An egg box holds 6 eggs. How many full egg boxes will there be?

c Fred reads 4 pages a day. His book has 35 pages. How many days will he take to read the whole book?

d A roll of material measures 14m. How many 3m lengths can be cut?

 *Some divisions aren't exact, they leave a remainder. 8 ÷ 3 = 2 remainder 2
You need to make a decision whether to round up or round down for division problems.*

Examples:
A tube holds 3 tennis balls. How many tubes are needed for 8 balls? 3 tubes are needed (one will have two tennis balls in it).
8 cakes are shared equally between 3 people. How many will each get? 2 cakes each, with 2 left over.

Challenge

Write each of the division facts for three times tables, choosing from ÷2, ÷3, ÷4, ÷5, ÷10, on 30 separate cards. Write the answers on the back of each card.

Shuffle them and lay them in a pile face up. Set a timer and see how many facts you can answer correctly in 30 seconds. Check each answer as you go along.

Keep a record of the number you get right and then after a few days see if you can beat your best score.

Brain Teaser

Class 4 has 30 children. The teacher wants to put the class into teams. How many different ways are there to divide the class into equal-sized teams?

2	groups of	15	children
	groups of		children
	groups of		children
	groups of		children
	groups of		children
	groups of		children

CALCULATING

2D shapes

A 2D shape is a flat shape. Look at the number of sides of each shape to help learn their names.

Triangle – 3 sides    Pentagon – 5 sides

Quadrilateral – 4 sides.    Hexagon – 6 sides

A circle, semi-circle and oval are shapes with curved sides.

Exercise 1

Sort these shapes. Draw them in the correct part of the Carroll diagram.

quadrilateral	not a quadrilateral

Exercise 2

Name these shapes. Draw a spot on each right angle.

a

b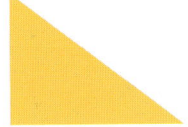

c

_____   _____   _____

 **Top Tip** Some shapes have right angles, which is a quarter of a whole turn.

For example, a rectangle has four right angles.

Exercise 3

Join each half shape to its matching full shape.

Challenge

Cut out a square and draw three straight lines at any angle across the square.

Cut along the lines and shuffle up the pieces.

Can you put the square back together again?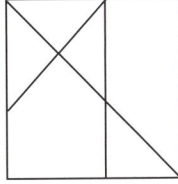

Can you use any two pieces to make a triangle? Three pieces?

Can you make a pentagon?

Make different shapes with your pieces.

Brain Teaser

How many triangles can you see in this shape?

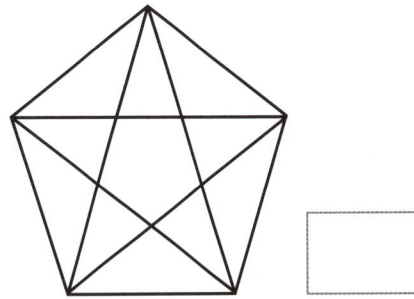

Be careful – some triangles can overlap.

3D shapes

UNDERSTANDING SHAPE

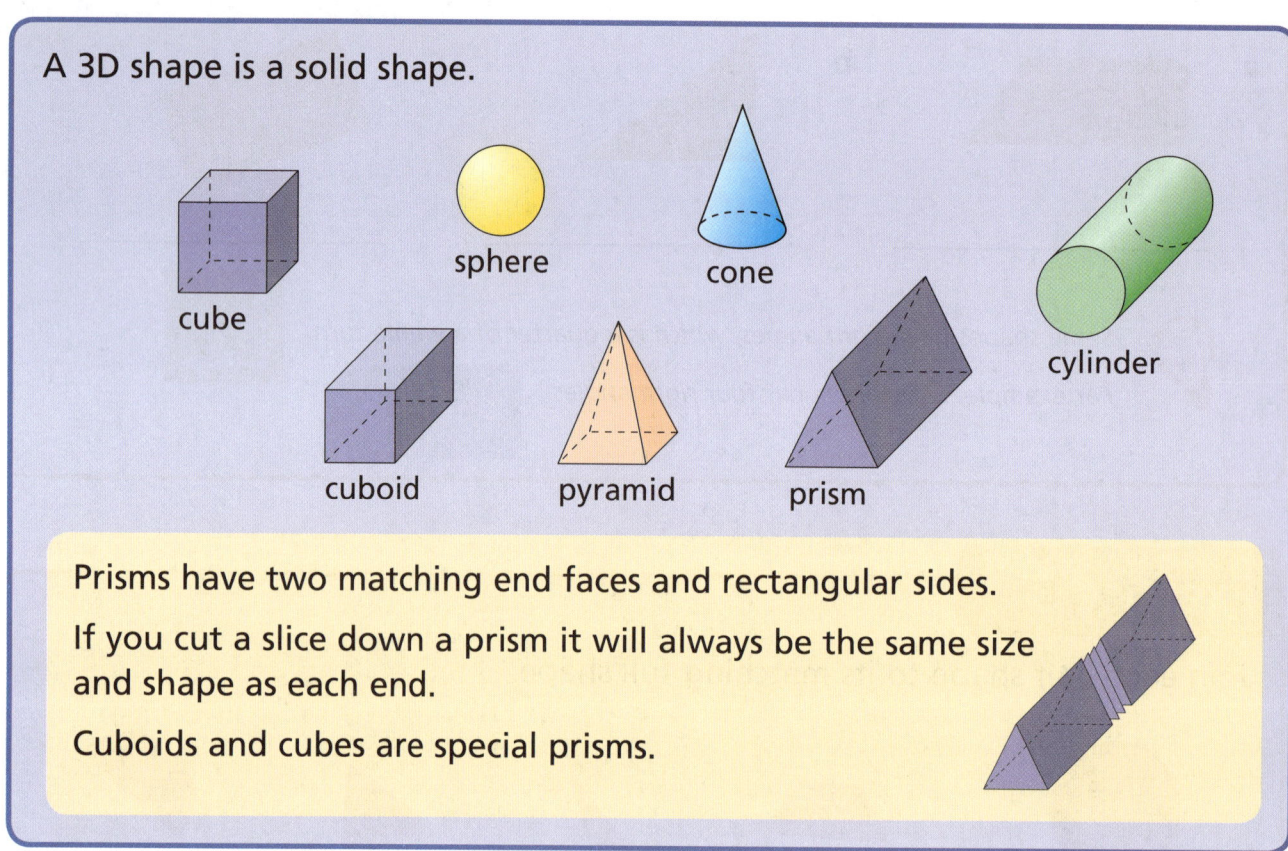

A 3D shape is a solid shape.

cube, sphere, cone, cylinder, cuboid, pyramid, prism

Prisms have two matching end faces and rectangular sides.

If you cut a slice down a prism it will always be the same size and shape as each end.

Cuboids and cubes are special prisms.

Exercise 1

Circle the odd one out in each set. Write the name of the shapes in each set.

a Name: _____

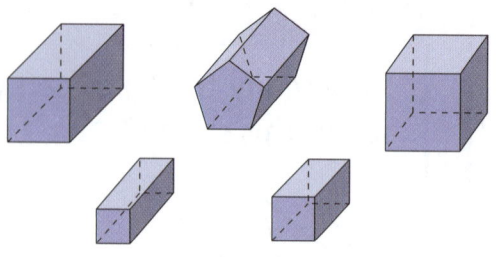

b Name: _____

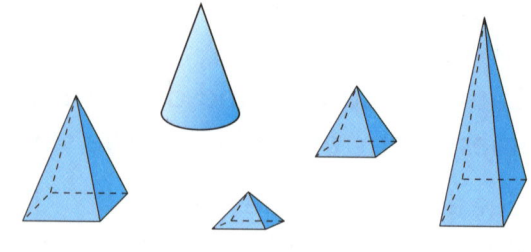

c Name: _____

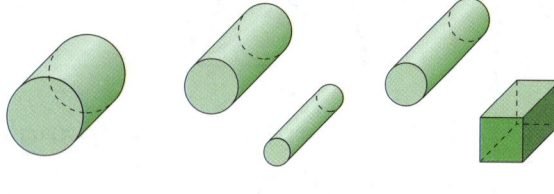

d Name: _____

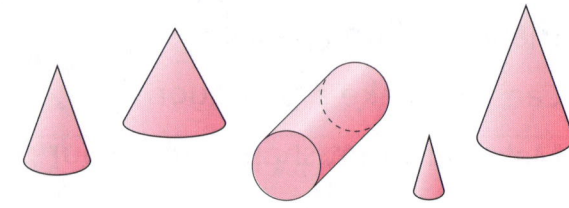

Exercise 2

Write true or false.

a A cuboid has a triangular face. _____

b A prism always has some rectangular or square faces. _____

c A sphere has no edges. _____

d A pyramid always has some rectangular or square faces. _____

e A pyramid has mainly triangular faces. _____

 **Top Tip** There are three main parts to 3D shapes.

This pyramid has 5 faces, 8 edges and 5 vertices.

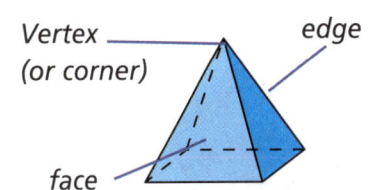

Exercise 3

Sort these shapes. Write the shape letter in the correct part of the Venn diagram.

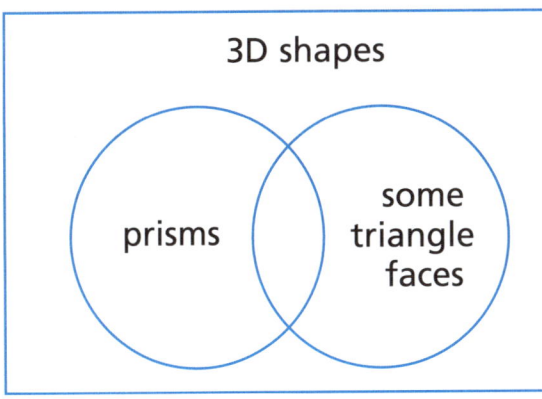

a 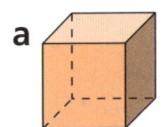 b  c  d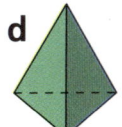

e 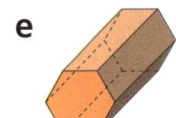 f 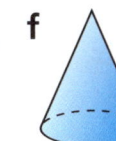 g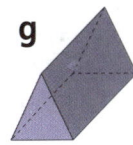

Challenge

Next time you finish a cereal box, open it out carefully. Undo all the flaps and then lay it out flat. Sketch it onto a piece of paper.

Open up other boxes in the same way and draw them so they can be compared.

These are called 'nets'.

Brain Teaser

How many faces, edges and vertices do each of these prisms have?

faces			
edges			
vertices			

UNDERSTANDING SHAPE

Reflective symmetry

A line of **symmetry** is like a mirror line.

One half of the shape looks like a reflection of the other half.

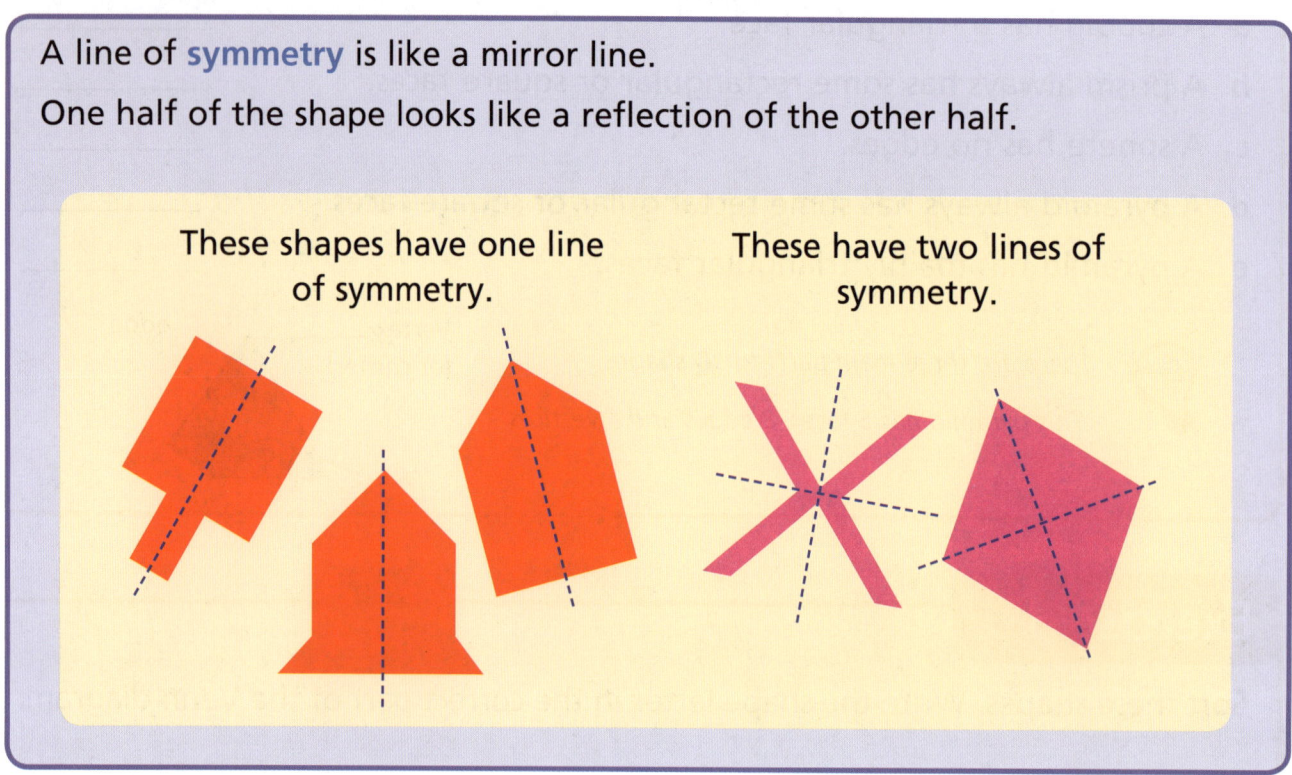

These shapes have one line of symmetry.

These have two lines of symmetry.

Exercise 1

Draw one line of symmetry on each shape.

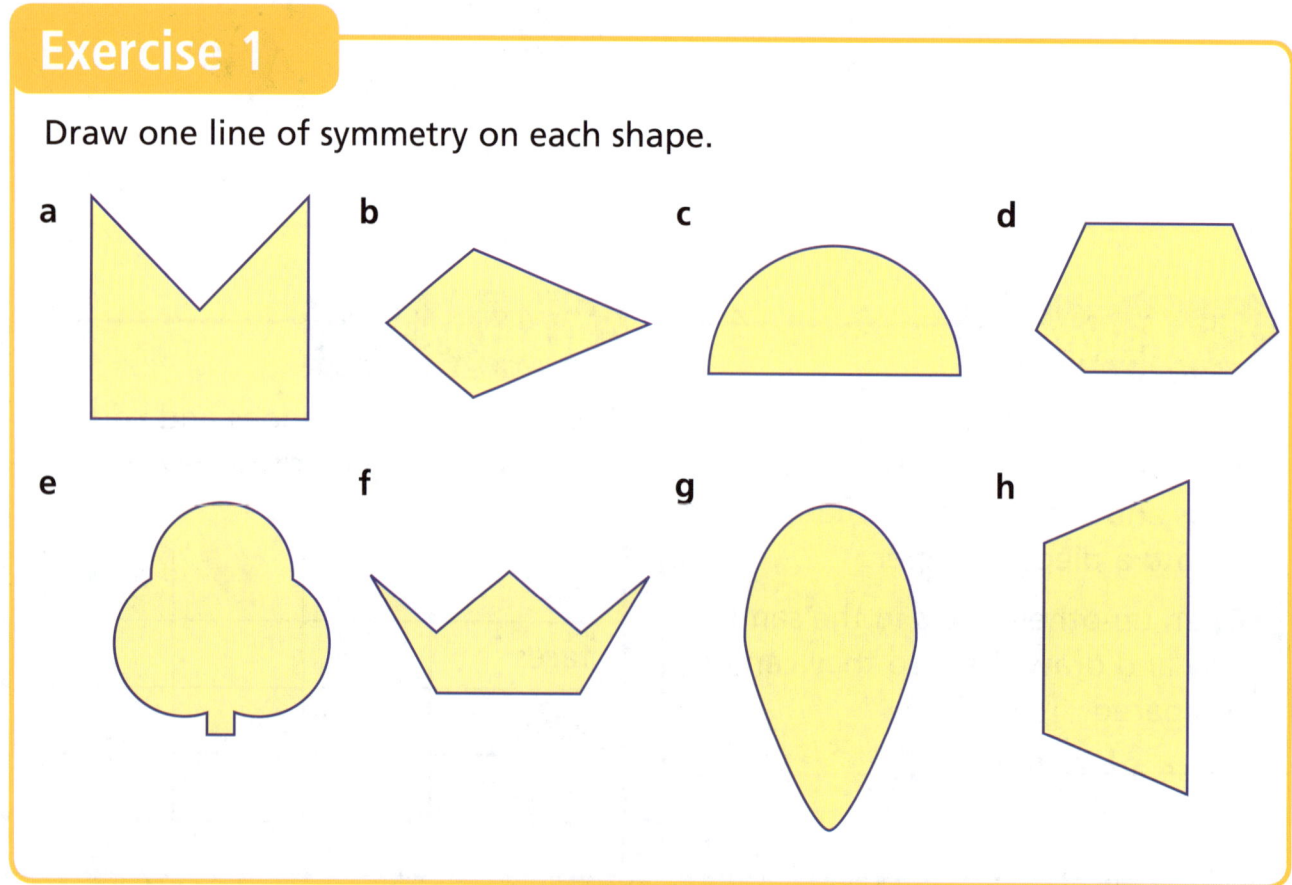

Exercise 2

Draw the reflection of each shape.

a

b

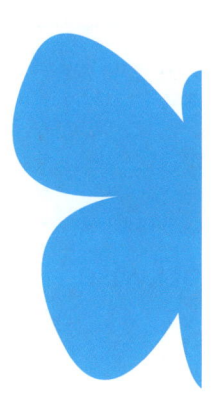

Exercise 3

Draw two lines of symmetry on these shapes.

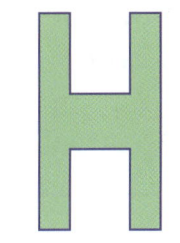

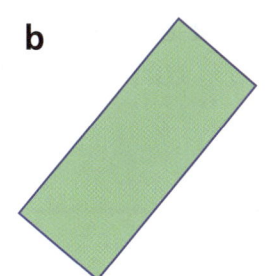

a   b   c

Top Tip: Lines of symmetry are not always up and down or side to side. Sometimes they are sloping. Try testing some of the shapes on this page with a small mirror. Place it along the mirror line and the shape in the mirror should be the same as the shape behind it.

Challenge

Fold a piece of paper in half. Cut out any shape along the fold line. Open out the shape and the fold line should be its line of symmetry.

Try different cuts and make a display of symmetrical shapes.

Using folding and cutting, how can you cut out shapes with two lines of symmetry?

Brain Teaser

Which of these is a reflection of the first pattern? Tick the correct tile.

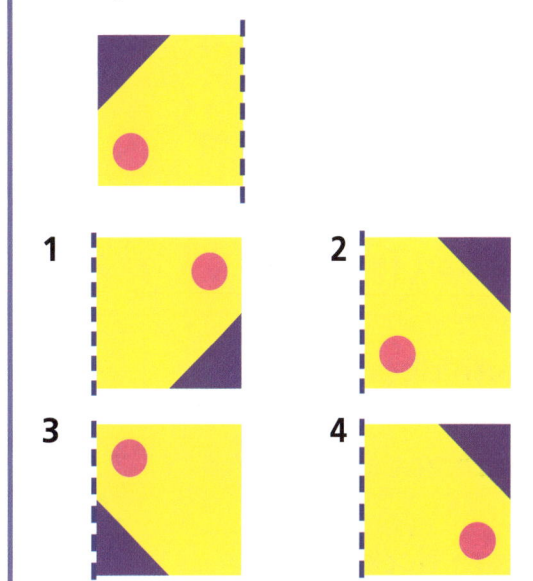

1   2

3   4

UNDERSTANDING SHAPE

Directions and angles

Check that you know these:

Clockwise   Anticlockwise

Left   Right

Four compass directions: N, W, E, S

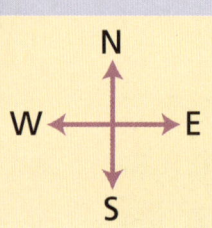

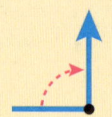

1 right-angle = $\frac{1}{4}$ turn

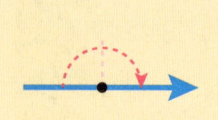

2 right-angles = $\frac{1}{2}$ turn

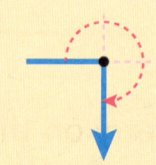

3 right-angles = $\frac{3}{4}$ turn

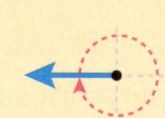

4 right-angles = 1 turn

Exercise 1

Which direction will you end up facing each time?

Always start facing North

a $\frac{1}{4}$ turn clockwise ➡

b $\frac{1}{2}$ turn anticlockwise ➡

c $\frac{1}{4}$ turn anticlockwise ➡

Always start facing East

d $\frac{3}{4}$ turn clockwise ➡

e $\frac{1}{4}$ turn anticlockwise ➡

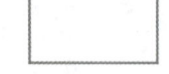

f $\frac{1}{2}$ turn clockwise ➡

Always start facing West

g $\frac{1}{4}$ turn anticlockwise ➡

h $\frac{3}{4}$ turn anticlockwise ➡

i $\frac{1}{4}$ turn clockwise ➡

Top Tip: When you need to turn left or right, remember to face in the correct direction before turning. If you get in a muddle between lefts and rights try this:

Look at the back of your hands and stretch out your thumbs. The left hand looks like the letter L.

Exercise 2

Follow the routes. Where does each car park?

a. forward 2 → turn right → forward 2 → turn left → forward 2 → turn left → forward 2 → turn right → forward 2 → BAY ☐

b. forward 4 → turn right → forward 2 → turn left → forward 2 → BAY ☐

c. forward 1 → turn left → forward 2 → turn right → forward 3 → turn right → forward 1 → turn left → forward 2 → BAY ☐

d. forward 3 → turn left → forward 2 → turn left → forward 1 → turn left → forward 1 → turn left → forward 4 → BAY ☐

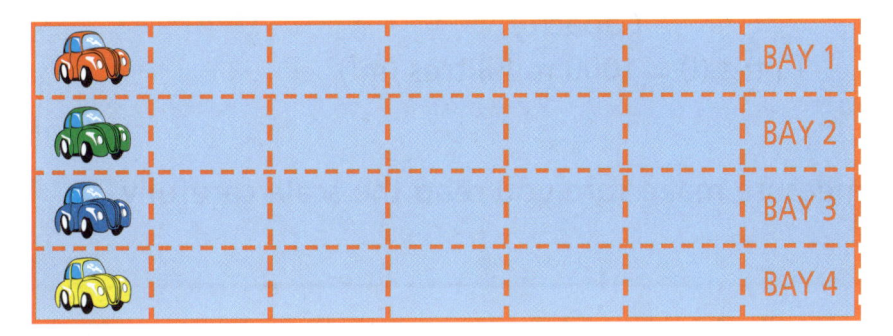

BAY 1
BAY 2
BAY 3
BAY 4

Challenge

Set up a mystery course in your classroom or home. Mark a starting point with an object, such as a chair, and use paces and turns to give someone directions to follow, to get back to the starting point.

For example:

START → 3 paces forward → quarter turn clockwise → 2 paces forward → three-quarter turn anti-clockwise → 4 paces forward → quarter turn clockwise → 2 paces forward → quarter turn clockwise → 1 pace forward → FINISH

Brain Teaser

Tick the right angle in each set.

1.

2.

3.

Measurement

Try to learn these different units of measurement.

Length
1 metre (m) = 100 centimetres (cm)
1 kilometre (km) = 1000 metres (m)

Weight
1 kilogram (kg) = 1000 grams (g)

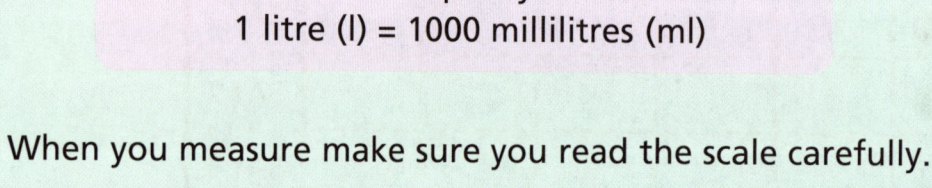

Capacity
1 litre (l) = 1000 millilitres (ml)

When you measure make sure you read the scale carefully.

Exercise 1

Use a ruler to measure these lines.

a _____ ☐ cm

b _____ ☐ cm

c _____ ☐ cm

d _____ ☐ cm

e _____ ☐ cm

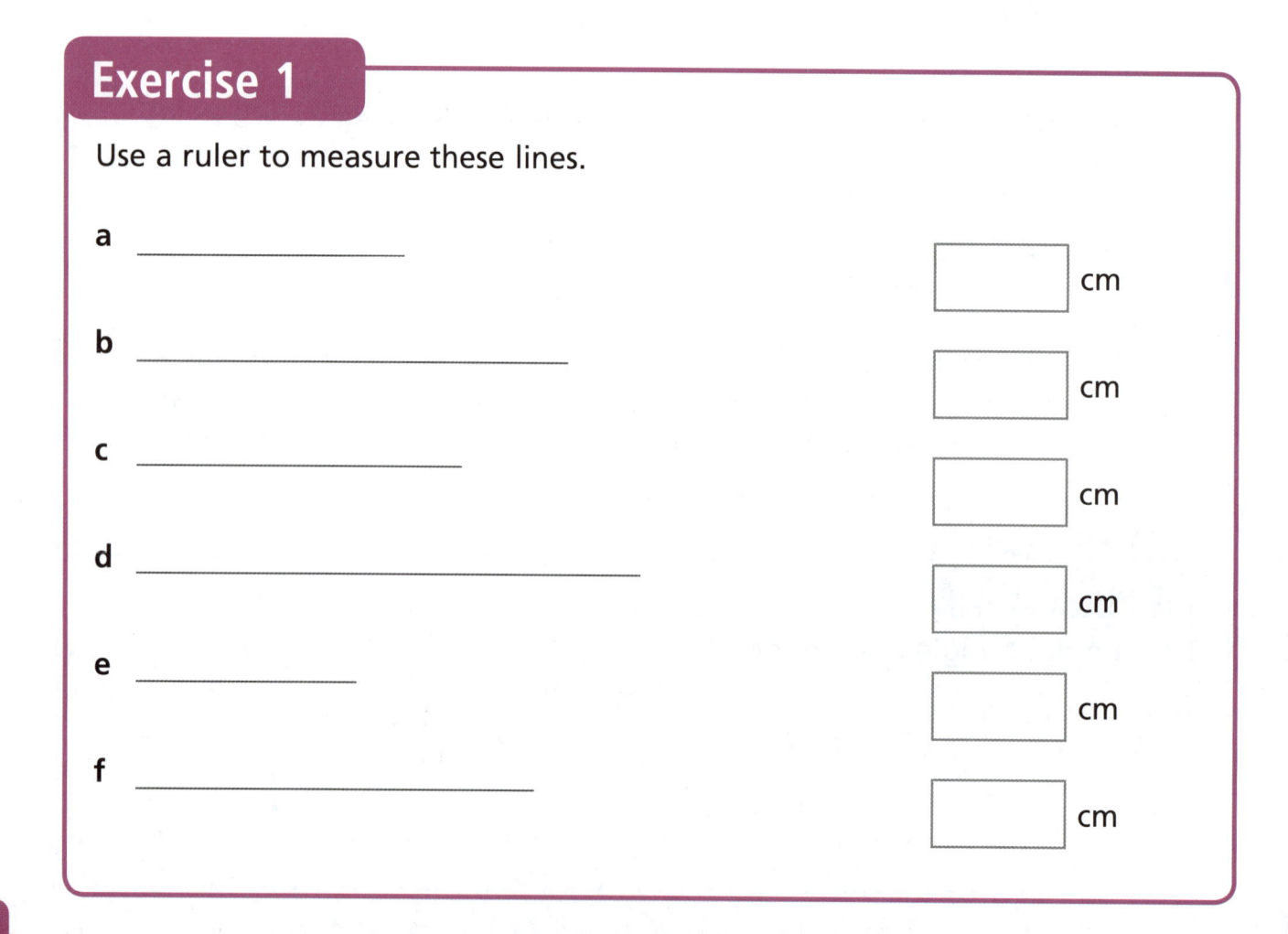

f _____ ☐ cm

Exercise 2

Write the measures shown.

a) ☐ ml

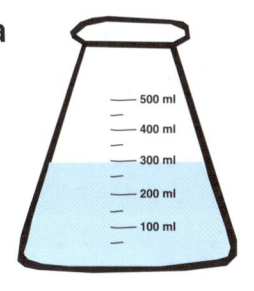

b) ☐ ml

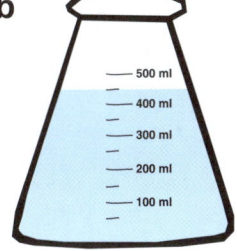

c) ☐ ml

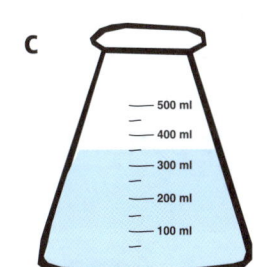

d) ☐ ml

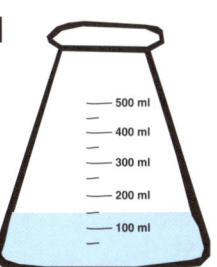

e) ☐ ml

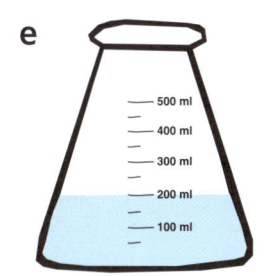

Top Tip: *Decimal points are used in measures and can be confusing, so look at them carefully.*

3.5m = 3 metres 50cm = 350cm

3.05m = 3 metres 5cm = 305cm

The decimal point separates the whole unit from the fraction of the unit.

Challenge

Try playing this measuring game with a friend. Shout out a length, say 6cm. Now try and draw a line 6cm long – without a ruler. How close are you?

Give a point for every $\frac{1}{2}$ centimetre that you were away from 6cm – the lower the score, the better. Shout out five other lengths, draw, measure, then score. Keep a tally of your score.

You've done really well if you score below 5 points!

Brain Teaser

The perimeter is the distance all around the edge of a shape.

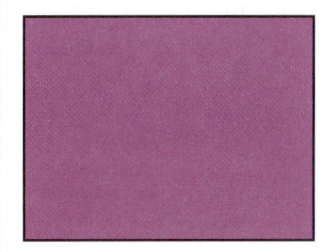

Estimate the perimeter of this rectangle.

Estimate = ☐ cm

Measure the perimeter.

Measure = ☐ cm

MEASURING

41

Reading the time

Clocks and watches use numbers or hands to show the time. To make it simple to read the time with any type of clock, read the hour first and then the minutes past the hour.

07:20

20 minutes past 7

Seven Twenty

04:35

35 minutes past 4

Four Thirty-five

Exercise 1

Write the times for these.

a

b

c

d

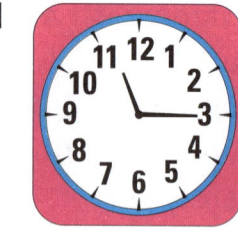

_____ _____ _____ _____

e

f

g

h

_____ _____ _____ _____

Exercise 2

Answer these time questions.

a How many minutes are there in a quarter of an hour? _____

b How many minutes are there in 2 hours? _____

c How many seconds are there in half a minute? _____

d Which month comes before September? _____

Top Tip Try to learn these:

1 minute = 60 seconds

1 hour = 60 minutes

1 day = 24 hours

1 week = 7 days

1 year = 12 months
= 52 weeks
= 365 days

Exercise 3

Draw the missing minute hands on these clocks.

a 7.45

b 10.25

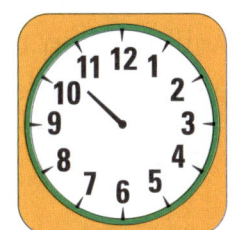

c 2.50

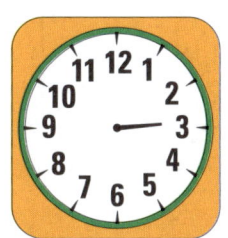

d 12.35

Challenge

Hickory, dickory, dock! Let's make a clock!

Make a 'tocker timer'.

1 Put blu-tac on a coffee jar lid.

2 Stick a card with the numbers of a clock onto blu-tac to make a 'face'.

3 Set the lid 'tocking' by setting it rolling.

Can you make the time go quicker, or slower?

Brain Teaser

In this Clockmaker's shop, all the clocks are telling the wrong time. Draw hands on the blank clock to show the real time.

20 minutes fast

50 minutes slow

25 minutes slow

Actual time:

MEASURING

Graphs and charts

HANDLING DATA

Information can be shown in lots of different ways, using graphs, charts, tables and diagrams. With each type, read all the different parts carefully to understand it.

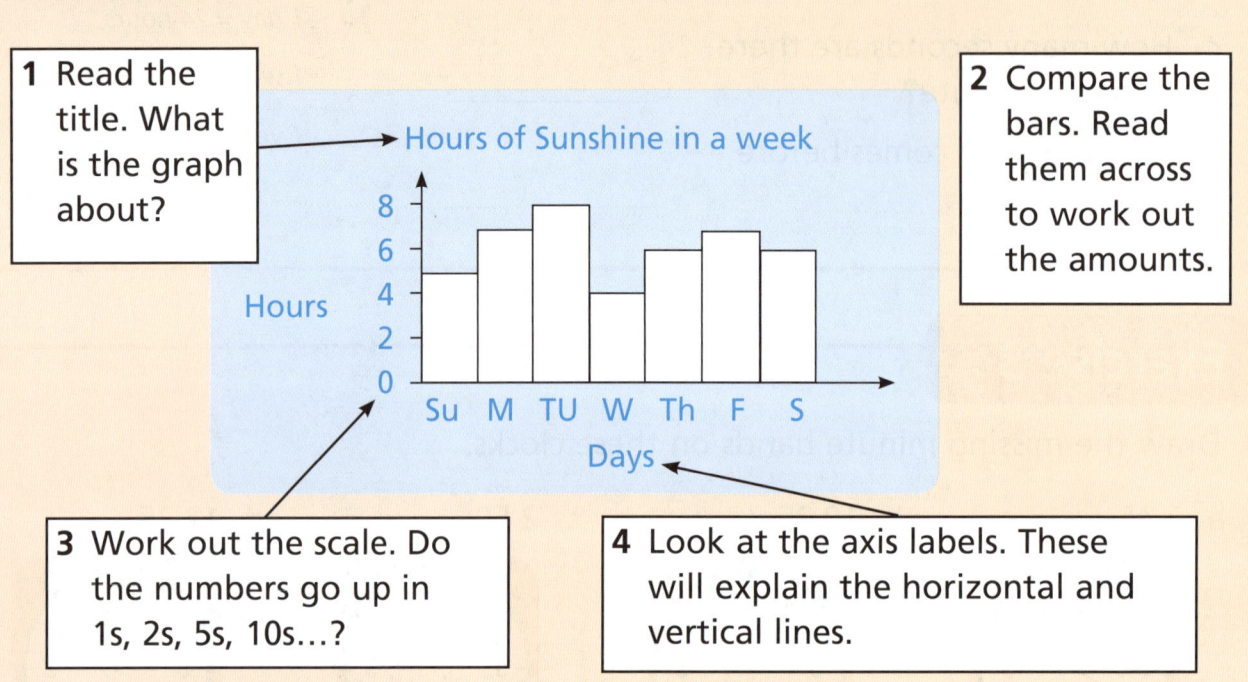

1 Read the title. What is the graph about?

Hours of Sunshine in a week

2 Compare the bars. Read them across to work out the amounts.

3 Work out the scale. Do the numbers go up in 1s, 2s, 5s, 10s…?

4 Look at the axis labels. These will explain the horizontal and vertical lines.

Exercise 1

Stickers collected by a group of children.

Stickers collected

a How many stickers did Lara collect?

b Who collected 35 stickers?

c How many more stickers has Tom collected than Ali?

d How many stickers have Javed and Millie collected altogether?

e How many more stickers does Lara need to collect to have 80?

44

Exercise 2

This pictogram shows the number of people on coaches at different times of the day.

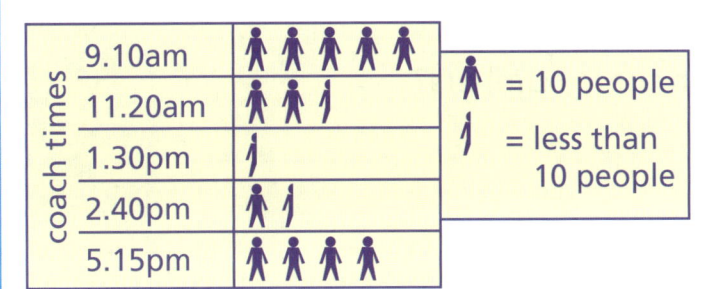

coach times	
9.10am	👤👤👤👤
11.20am	👤👤👣
1.30pm	👣
2.40pm	👤👣
5.15pm	👤👤👤👤

👤 = 10 people
👣 = less than 10 people

Top Tip: *Pictograms are graphs made up from pictures. The important thing is to find out what each small picture stands for. Look at the key. For example, for this pictogram, one picture stands for 10 people. It means that some answers will be approximate. Half a person could be 3 or 9 – or any number less than 10.*

a How many people were on the 5.15pm coach?

b Which coach had 17 people travelling on it?

c How many more people were on the 9.10am coach than on the 5.15pm coach?

d Approximately how many more people were on the 2.40pm coach than the 1.30pm coach?

e Approximately how many people travelled on the coaches in total through the day?

Challenge

What's your favourite TV program? Carry out a survey of favourite types of TV programmes with your family, friends or at school.

You need to make up a list of types of programme for them to choose. Some examples to start you off are cartoons, news, sport, quiz…

Draw a graph or pictogram to show your results. Which is the most popular type? Which is the least popular?

Brain Teaser

Sam: My cat is black. My front door is not blue.

Ruth: My cat is not white. My front door is yellow.

Jack: My cat is white. My front door is not red.

Write the children's names in the chart to show the information.

house number	black cat	ginger cat	white cat
1			
2			
3			

HANDLING DATA

45

Test practice

1 What is the difference between these numbers?

17   8

☐

2 Write 401 in words.

_____

Tonight's film STARTS
MATHS MASTER MOVIE

3 What time does the film start?

_____

4 The film is on for 1 hour 30 minutes.
What time does it finish?

_____

5 Name this shape.

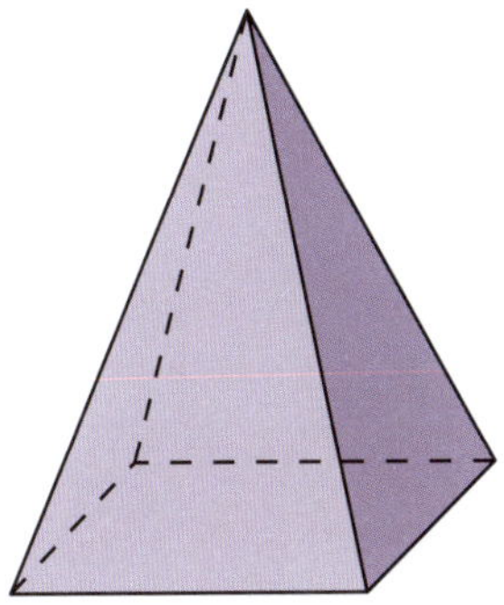

_____

6 A newspaper costs 55p. How much change will be given from £1?

_____

7 What is 19 more than 25?

_____

8 What is the next number in this sequence?

14 17 20 23 26 ☐

9 What is 1.5m in centimetres?

_____

10 What is the missing number?

25	40	65
30		95
35	40	75

11 Draw a line of symmetry on the shape.

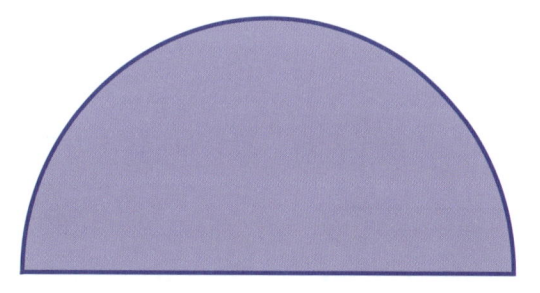

12 What is the next odd number after 79?

_____

13 Arrange these three digits to make the smallest possible number.

| 5 | 8 | 4 |

_____

14 Now arrange the digits to make a number as near as possible to 500.

_____

15 What is the weight of this parcel?

_____

16 Three drinks cost 30p each. What change will there be from £1?

_____

17 Name this 2D shape.

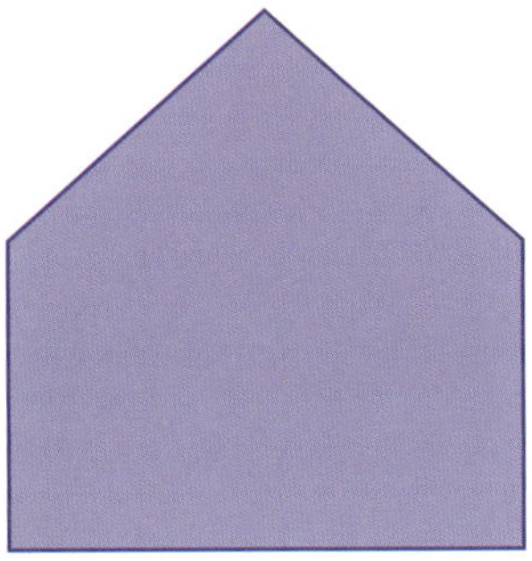

_____

18 Tick the right-angles on the shape.

score

19 What is half of 24?

_____

20 8 × 3 = ☐

21 How much is in this jug?

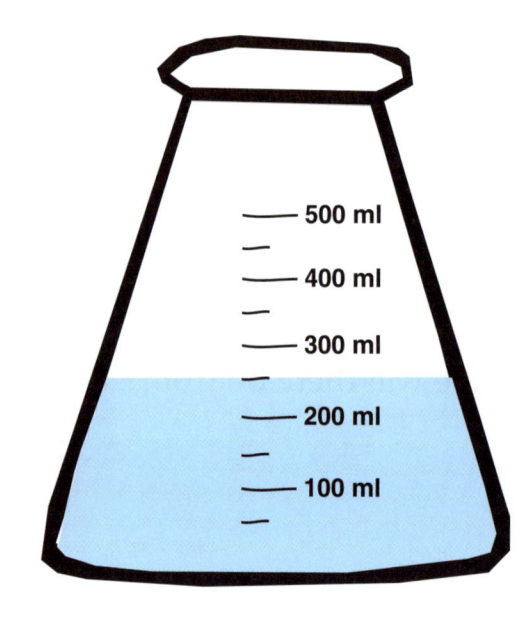

_____

22 Tick the shapes that have $\frac{1}{4}$ shaded.

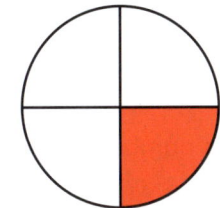

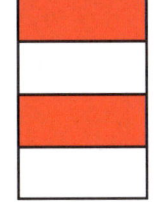

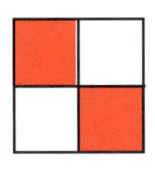

a ☐   b ☐   c ☐   d ☐

23 What number is the arrow pointing to?

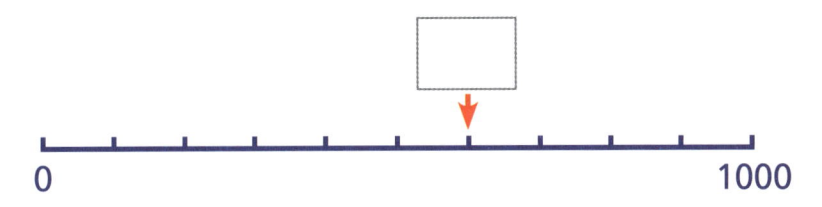

24 35 − ☐ = 18

25 Circle the numbers that divide exactly by 3.

22   18   26   21   16   27

Glossary

Carroll diagram a grid used to sort things into groups or sets

column a vertical line going up or down

change the amount of money you are given back if you pay more than the price of an item. If £5 was given for an item costing £4.50, you would have 50p change

compare when you compare two objects or numbers you look for differences and similarities between them

decimal point used to show which digits are whole numbers and which are fractions. The digits to the left of the decimal point give the number of ones, tens and hundreds. The digits to the right of the decimal point give the number of tenths, hundredths, and so on.

With money, the decimal point separates the pounds from the pence

denominator is the number below the line in a fraction. It shows how many parts a whole shape or number of items is divided into.
e.g. $\frac{1}{4}$ of 12. The denominator is 4, so $\frac{1}{4}$ of 12 is $12 \div 4 = 3$

difference the difference is the number you must count on to get from a smaller number to a bigger one. You can also work it out by subtracting the smaller one from the bigger one. e.g. The difference between 4 and 9 is 5

digit is any of the ten numerals: 0, 1, 2, 3, 4, 5, 6, 7, 8 or 9. Numbers are made up from digits

fraction a number that is part of a whole number. They can be written in different ways: $\frac{1}{4}$, $\frac{3}{5}$ and 0.9 are all fractions. 0.9 is a decimal fraction

prism a solid shape with matching end shapes, such as triangles, squares or hexagons. The faces joining these end shapes are always rectangles

remainder if a number cannot be divided exactly by another number, it can leave a remainder or an amount left over. 11 divided by 2 is 5 with 1 as a remainder

row a horizontal line of objects or numbers going across

rounding comparing a number to the nearest ten. A 'round number' is a number ending in zero: 10, 20, 30, 40, 50, 60, 70, 80, 90 or 100

sequence a list of numbers which usually have a pattern. They are often numbers written in order

symmetry when two halves of a shape or pattern are identical

Glossary

trio a set of three items. A multiplication and division trio are a set of three numbers, such as 4, 5 and 20, that can make four facts:
4 × 5 = 20, 5 × 4 = 20, 20 ÷ 4 = 5, 20 ÷ 5 = 4.

Addition and subtraction trios work in the same way: 4, 6 and 10 are a trio: 4 + 6 = 10, 6 + 4 = 1 0, 10 − 6 = 4, 10 − 4 = 6

Venn diagram a way of showing how different things can be sorted into groups. The groups are known as sets

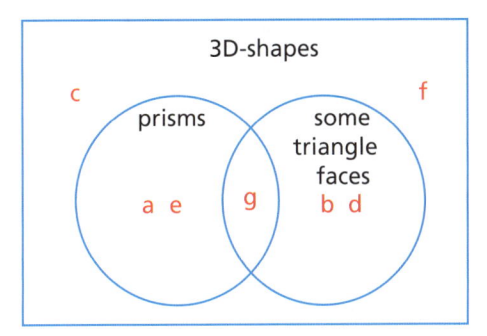

```
3D-shapes
c                              f
    prisms      some
                triangle
                faces
      a e    g    b d
```

Speaking and listening

Speaking

Having a conversation is all about taking turns. You need to think carefully about what you say, to make sure that the person you are speaking to will understand you. Then you must listen to their reply, so that you know what to say next.

Taking turns and listening is not just good manners. If you don't do it, you might as well be talking to yourself!

Remember, too, that the kind of information you get back from the person you are speaking to will depend on the questions you ask. Try to ask questions that need a full sentence in reply, rather than just 'yes' or 'no'.

"Are you happy?"　　"Yes!"

"Why are you happy?"　"I'm happy because it's my birthday and I'm having a party!"

Listening

Most of us are terrible listeners! Watching TV and playing computer games encourages us to use our eyes, not our ears! It is very easy to focus too much on what you have to say, and not give enough attention to what the person you are speaking to is saying. You can practise listening skills by playing games like Chinese Whispers, where you whisper a message from person to person around the group. Unless everyone listens really carefully, the message that gets to the end of the group won't be right!

You can also throw a ball backwards and forwards as you speak to a partner. When you are holding the ball, it is your turn to speak. When your partner has it, you have to listen.

For a real challenge, play the alphabet game. One player starts by saying 'I went to the shops and I bought...' before adding something beginning with the letter A. The next player must repeat what the first player said, before adding something starting with B, and so on. Can you get right through the alphabet without forgetting what other players have bought?

Exercise 1

Speaking

Look at these questions. Circle the ones which will help to keep a conversation going by requiring a longer answer than just 'yes' or 'no'.

a Do you like playing football?

b What kinds of films do you like?

c Why do you think Mrs Brown is so cheerful today?

d Is it raining?

e Do you want to play tennis?

f How do you send an email from this computer?

Exercise 2

Listening

Now see how well you can listen. Ask a helper to gather five everyday objects, without letting you see them. Get your helper to describe what each object looks, feels and smells like. Can you guess what each one is?

Use the table to record useful clue words and what you think each object is.

Object	Useful clue words	I think the object is…
1		
2		
3		
4		
5		

Challenge

Some things are harder to say than others. Tongue-twisters are a great way to practise saying tricky things! Try this one: Around the ragged rock, the ragged rascal ran!

Brain Teaser

Ask a partner about one of these topics. Listen carefully to their opinion. Do you agree?

What do you think about school uniform?

How much homework should children get?

SPEAKING AND LISTENING

Prefixes

Prefixes are letters that can be added to the beginning of words. *Pre* means before. It tells us that a prefix comes at the beginning of the word.

Pre is a prefix itself. Think of the words preview, prehistoric and premature. If you don't know what they mean, look them up in a dictionary!

Prefixes give us clues to the meanings of words. If we know what the prefix means, it can help us to understand new words.

For example, *anti* means against. Antidote means medicine used against a poison. Anti-slavery means against, or opposed to, slavery.

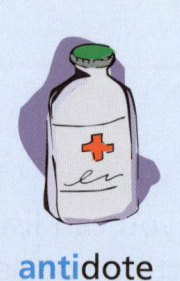

prehistoric

antidote

Exercise 1

Underline the prefix for each of these words.

a unacceptable

b retake

c misunderstanding

d non-flammable

e anti-inflammatory

f prepay

g ex-president

h prefabricate

i inaccurate

j non-smoker

Top Tip

Prefixes can also be used to make new words that have the opposite meaning of the original word:

mis (prefix) + lead = mislead
non (prefix) + sense = nonsense

Exercise 2

Add the prefix *non* or *mis* to these words to make a new word!

a _____ perishable
b _____ understand
c _____ refundable
d _____ inform
e _____ stop
f _____ conductor
g _____ fiction
h _____ behave

Exercise 3

Read the explanation of each word. Then use the correct prefix from the box to complete the words.

pre   un   anti   in   mis   non

a _____ historic – before the days recorded by history.

b _____ action – no action.

c _____ understand – not understand.

d _____ sense – making no sense; silly.

e _____ clockwise – moves the other way to clockwise.

f _____ used – not used.

Challenge

Find out about more prefixes, by reading through a newspaper article and underlining all the prefixes you can find.

Brain Teaser

Change these words to mean the opposite of the original meaning by adding a prefix.

1 _____ understanding
2 _____ sense
3 _____ sensitive
4 _____ happy
5 _____ behave

WORD STRUCTURE AND SPELLING

Homonyms and homophones

Homonyms are words that have the same spelling, but mean different things. You can only tell what they mean by looking at the context of the word in the sentence.

> Wave can mean:
>
> gesture   motion   shape

Homophones are words that are pronounced alike, but have different meanings or spellings.

> to, too and two
>
> which   witch
> ?

Exercise 1

Match the homonyms to their meanings. Join them with a line.

a Animal skin

b A grand event where people dance

c Something that you chew

d Round toy

e Keep out of sight

f Something that keeps your teeth in place

gum

ball

hide

Exercise 2

Circle the correct word in each sentence. Careful, it's trickier than it looks!

a I'll isle aisle open the door!

b That's really naughty. It's not aloud allowed.

c The alter altar is at the front of the church.

d Spiders have eight ate legs.

e The sun's shining in my I eye aye.

f I kicked the ball bawl.

Top Tip *Have a look at a comic or magazine or newspaper. Underline all of the homonyms on one page. Now see if you can find any homophones.*

Exercise 3

Read the description and circle the word being described.

a A woolly animal that eats grass.   ewe   you   yew

b Something that makes my cat itch!   flee   flea

c The part of Sam's sock that wears out first!   heel   heal

d A noise Mel makes when she has to go to bed.   grown   groan

Challenge

Homonym or homophone? You decide!

1 board and bored

   _____

2 buy, by and bye

   _____

3 chews and choose

   _____

4 currant and current

   _____

Brain Teaser

Underline the correct word.

1 If she seas/sees/seize the mouse, she will scream!

2 Which sighed/side of the paper shall I write on?

3 What are their/there/they're names?

4 I want to/two/too go shopping.

WORD STRUCTURE AND SPELLING

Contractions

Contractions are where letters are dropped from words and an apostrophe is added to show that letters are missing.

could not	did not	would not	is not
⬇	⬇	⬇	⬇
couldn't	didn't	wouldn't	isn't

Exercise 1

Write down the shortened, contracted form of these words.

a   must not ➔ _____

b   cannot ➔ _____

c   is not ➔ _____

d   should not ➔ _____

e   has not ➔ _____

f   you are ➔ _____

g   I have ➔ _____

h   he has ➔ _____

i   have not ➔ _____

Exercise 2

Change these contractions into the longer versions of the words.

a won't _____

b can't _____

c she's _____

d he'll _____

e we've _____

f they'll _____

g hasn't _____

h you're _____

Exercise 3

Write this passage again, changing all of the contractions into the longer versions of the words.

> I don't want to go to the park today. It's boring. My brother hasn't been for ages either. He says there's nowhere to play football.

_____
_____
_____
_____
_____

Top Tip: Contractions are used in dialogue or informal writing, such as letters to friends. They should not be used in formal writing.

Challenge

Underline the contractions in these sentences and write the full versions of the words below each sentence.

1 I wouldn't like to go.
   _____

2 The cat won't go outside.
   _____

3 I can't do it!
   _____

Brain Teaser

Write the contractions for these words.

1 I have _____

2 we will _____

3 should not _____

4 is not _____

WORD STRUCTURE AND SPELLING

Suffixes

Suffixes are collections of letters that can be added to the end of words.
Suffixes like *ly*, *able*, *ing*, *ful*, *like*, *ic* and *worthy* can often be added to nouns to make **adjectives**.

> hope (noun) + ful = hopeful (adjective)
> like (noun) + able = likeable (adjective)
> news (noun) + worthy = newsworthy (adjective)

Remember, an adjective is a describing word. It describes a **noun**.

Exercise 1

Look at the words below. Next to each one, write down the correct suffix from the box. Then write out the new word that it makes.

> able   ful   ic   ly   worthy

a kind + _____ = _____

b play + _____ = _____

c hero + _____ = _____

d love + _____ = _____

e blame + _____ = _____

Top Tip: Look back to page 4 to remind yourself about prefixes. Remember, a prefix goes at the beginning of an existing word. A suffix goes at the end. An existing word can have a prefix and a suffix, for example <u>un</u>hero<u>ic</u>.

Exercise 2

Write the suffix *ish* or *ful* next to each word to make an adjective.

a baby_____
b child_____
c dread_____
d hope_____
e mourn_____
f wonder_____
g wish_____
h self_____
i boy_____
j tear_____

Exercise 3

Tick the words which make a new word when the suffix *able* is added.

a shock_____ ☐
b like_____ ☐
c break_____ ☐
d hope_____ ☐
e enjoy_____ ☐
f road_____ ☐
g wash_____ ☐
h drink_____ ☐
i jump_____ ☐

Challenge

"I am hopeful that I won't be penniless after pocket money day!"

Underline the suffixes in this sentence.

Brain Teaser

Using the right suffix depends on the sense of the rest of the sentence. Cross out the word from the brackets that is not a real word!

1. The teacher says she gives me jobs to do because I am (trustworthy trustish).
2. That's (wishful wishworthy) thinking!
3. I am completely (penniable penniless) after all that shopping!

WORD STRUCTURE AND SPELLING

Spelling strategy 1

Look/say/cover/write/check is a great and easy way to learn new spellings!

Look at the shape of the word. **body**

Are there any tails, such as in *y*, or any sticks, such as in *d*? Are there any other shapes, such as *ee* or *oo*, in the middle of the word?

Say the word. It will help you to remember it. Sound out the syllables to yourself.

Cover the word. Can you remember the shape of the word without looking at it? Can you see any tails or sticks? Can you see any other shapes?

Write the word. Can you remember it? If there are letters you cannot remember, just write the ones you do remember and leave a space where you think any other letters should go.

Check the word. Uncover it. If it is not completely correct, put a tick above the letters you have got right and keep trying!

Another good way to learn spellings is to look for different words that contain the same sound. Sometimes you just change the first letter and you make a new word!

Exercise 1

Learn these words using look/say/cover/write/check.

- **a** different
- **b** below
- **c** write
- **d** playground
- **e** picture
- **f** remember
- **g** igloo
- **h** christmas

Exercise 2

Now learn these words. Careful, they might be tricky!

a change
b changing
c care
d careful
e carefully
f peace
g peaceful
h peacefully
i event
j eventful
k uneventful
l noisy
m noisily
n noisier

Exercise 3

Look at these words. Write down some new words by changing the first letter. An example has been done for you.

a bat _fat cat hat_
b ball _____
c rut _____
d dad _____
e big _____
f bin _____
g cake _____

Top Tip: *To learn how to spell long, hard words, split them into sound chunks or syllables. To work out where to split up words, put two fingers underneath your chin and say the word that you want to spell slowly. Get a pen and a piece of paper, and every time your chin drops when you say a sound, it is a part of the word (a syllable). Write the sounds down and it will help you to work out how to spell the word!*

Challenge

How many words can you make by changing the first letter of *mad*? Try adding more than one letter to make even more!

Brain Teaser

Write down all of the words you can make by changing the first letter of these words.

1 bid _____
2 bit _____
3 race _____

Spelling strategy 2

Looking for smaller words inside longer words is a great way of improving your spelling!

If you remember the small word and how to spell it, then that's a chunk of a longer, more complicated word you already know how to spell.

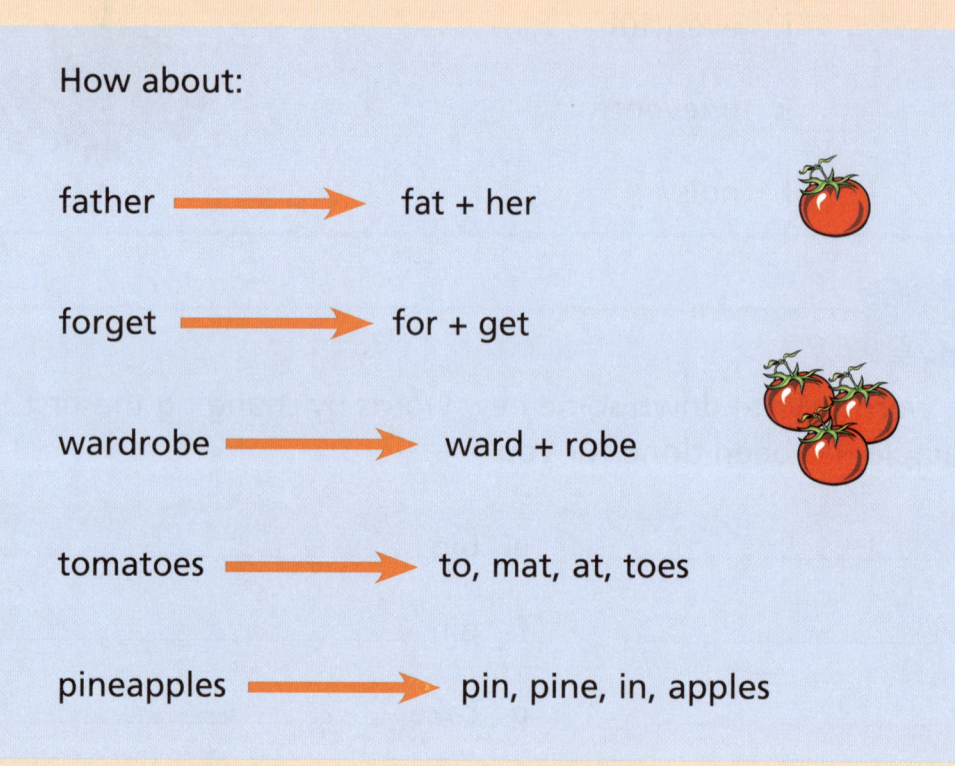

How about:

father ➡ fat + her

forget ➡ for + get

wardrobe ➡ ward + robe

tomatoes ➡ to, mat, at, toes

pineapples ➡ pin, pine, in, apples

Exercise 1

Find two smaller words inside each of these words, then write them down.

a lesson _____ _____

b abundance _____ _____

c history _____ _____

d shell _____ _____

e weather _____ _____

f exchange _____ _____

Exercise 2

Find three smaller words inside each of these longer words, then write them down.

a admittance _____ _____ _____

b electricity _____ _____ _____

c mustard _____ _____ _____

d pricey _____ _____ _____

e splendid _____ _____ _____

f standard _____ _____ _____

Exercise 3

Find four smaller words in each of these words, then write them down.

a another _____ _____ _____ _____

b archive _____ _____ _____ _____

c bulletin _____ _____ _____ _____

d airplane _____ _____ _____ _____

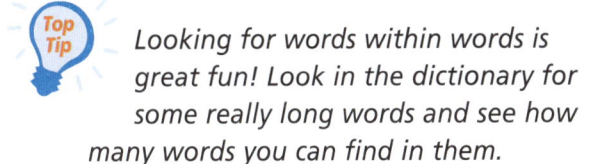

Top Tip: *Looking for words within words is great fun! Look in the dictionary for some really long words and see how many words you can find in them.*

Challenge

Does your name or nickname appear in any words? Or are there any words inside your name? Write them here:

Brain Teaser

Write down all of the smaller words you can find in the word **cartridge**.

WORD STRUCTURE AND SPELLING

Verbs

A **verb** is an action (or doing) word. You can make your own writing more interesting if you try to use a variety of verbs instead of using the same ones all of the time.

The girl was shouting (verb) because she saw a spider running (verb) up the wall.

This could be written as:

The girl was shrieking (verb) because she saw a spider scuttling (verb) up the wall.

The second sentence is much more exciting, because the verbs are more descriptive!

Exercise 1

Underline the verbs in these sentences.

a The boy is racing home.

b The bat is fluttering in the darkness.

c The mouse is squeaking.

d The girl is singing a beautiful song.

e I walked for miles in the hot sun.

f The sun is shining brightly.

Remember, a verb is often called a doing word, because it describes the action in a sentence.

Exercise 2

Look at these sets of words. Some mean the same thing, but there is an odd one out in each set. Draw a circle round the odd verb.

a giggle smile chuckle

b run sprint walk

c laugh grin smile

d cry weep frown

e drink sip eat

f dance jump leap

Exercise 3

Write your own verbs to complete these sentences. Try to think of something exciting!

a The cat _____ the mouse round the garden.

b The monster _____ at the children.

c Spiders are scary, because they _____ up and down on the ceiling.

d Stars are beautiful when they_____.

e The girl thought the clown was really funny and she was _____.

f The snake _____ across the rock.

Challenge

Verbs tell us about actions. Underline the verbs in these sentences.

1 The cat scratched my leg.
2 The bug climbed the wall.
3 The dog barked loudly.

Brain Teaser

Tick the verb in each set that you think is most exciting!

1 ☐ eat ☐ gobble ☐ chew

2 ☐ look ☐ watch ☐ observe

3 ☐ shout ☐ yell ☐ scream

SENTENCE STRUCTURE AND PUNCTUATION

Adjectives

Adjectives are often called describing words. They are what make your writing exciting, because you add lots of description!

Compare these two sentences:

1 I saw a spider.
2 I saw a huge, black, hairy spider.

The second sentence gives you a much clearer picture of a horrible spider!

Exercise 1

Underline the adjectives in each sentence.

a The slimy slug crawled up the wall.

b I bit the shiny, red apple.

c The elephant was enormous, grey and wrinkly.

d I hate smelly cheese!

e He was big, bad and ugly.

f The sparkling frost glittered in the moonlight.

g My cat is tabby.

Remember, adjectives make your work exciting, and a more exciting choice of adjectives makes your work even more exciting! Look through a magazine or comic and see if you agree.

Exercise 2

Underline the most powerful and descriptive adjective in each sentence.

a   The bath was warm/hot/scalding.

b   The dog was big/enormous/large.

c   The mouse was small/little/miniscule.

d   The story was amusing/hilarious/funny.

e   The wind was cold/freezing/icy.

Exercise 3

Look at the words in bold. Then, in the spaces, write a more exciting or interesting version.

a   The cat was **fierce**. _____

b   The horse was **big**. _____

c   The water was **cold**. _____

d   The lady was **pretty**. _____

e   The film was **good**. _____

f   The spider was **scary**. _____

g   The sun was **hot**. _____

Challenge

Choose the best adjective for each sentence.

1   Mel's tantrums are really bad/spectacular/big.

2   Mel's hair is really messy/untidy/bizarre.

3   Mel's voice is loud/noisy/ear shattering.

Brain Teaser

Underline the most exciting adjective in each pair.

1   The scorpion was huge/big.

2   The lion was ferocious/fierce.

3   The beetle was large/gigantic.

4   The water was scalding/hot.

Pronouns

A **pronoun** takes the place of a **noun**. A pronoun can also refer back to a noun. You must use the correct pronoun, so that your reader clearly understands which noun it refers to.

The most common pronouns are:

> I   you   he   she   it   me   they

Look at this example.

> Eleanor (noun) went to the pictures with Katie (noun).
> They (pronoun) bought some popcorn.

Pronouns must agree with the noun they replace or refer back to. If the noun is **singular** (there is only one), so is the pronoun.

> Lucy (noun) went to school.

Lucy is singular. So the correct pronoun would be *she*.

> She (singular pronoun) went to school.

Exercise 1

Match these nouns to their pronouns. Join them with a line.

a	the cat	it
b	Mrs Jones	he
c	Stephen	me
d	we	she
e	Granny and Grandad	us
f	I	they

Top Tip

*Remember: the words **everybody, anybody, anyone, each, neither, nobody, someone** and **a person** are singular and take singular pronouns.*

For example: Everybody ought to do his or her best.

Exercise 2

Draw a circle around the pronoun in each sentence. Careful! You may find more than one in some sentences.

a Bethany paid some money and she went into the concert.

b Simon and Peter like computer games. They play them all the time.

c Alex threw his sandwich away because he didn't like it.

d My cats play in the garden. They love pouncing on leaves!

e I like orange juice. It tastes great.

Exercise 3

Fill in the gaps to explain who the pronouns are about.

a David and Tina love playing football. They like to score goals!

   Who are "they"? _____ and _____

b I look after my horses carefully. I clean them out every weekend.

   Who are "them"? _____

c Ellie is three. She goes to nursery.

   Who is "she"? _____

Challenge

Here are some pronouns that people use a lot:

> I me he him she you they them her we us.

Underline the pronouns in these sentences. Be careful though. Sometimes there's more than one!

1 He said he would come at 3pm.

2 I thought you liked them!

3 Why can't she go?

Brain Teaser

Write a pronoun in the gaps.

1 Today is my birthday. _____ am eight today.

2 My brother and I went to the swimming baths. _____ enjoyed the slides!

3 There are lots of spiders in the cupboard. _____ give me the creeps!

Speech marks

Speech marks show us when someone is talking.

"We can't wait for the summer holidays!" said Hilary.

A speech bubble is another way of showing us that someone is talking.

This tastes great!

Exercise 1

Draw a line under the speech in these sentences. Then write down how you know it is speech.

a "It's time for school!" called mum.

b "We are going to the shops," replied Kevin.

c "Would you like to come to my party?" asked Holly.

d "I don't like sprouts!" the boy cried. "I want an ice-cream!"

e "Can you help me to open this jar?" asked Granny.

f "Would you like to borrow this book?" asked the librarian.

_____

_____

Top Tip: Don't forget, speech marks are only used when someone is actually speaking, not when their speech is being reported.

Exercise 2

Look at these sentences. Put speech marks in the correct places.

a Put on your wellies, Jo! called mum.

b Every time we go to the swimming baths, said Harvey, I get really cold.

c Stop that! shouted the teacher.

d You are such a good footballer! sighed the girl.

Exercise 3

Write what is being said in the speech bubbles into sentences using speech marks. Use the pictures to help you.

Stop! Don't run in school!

Ahh! Aren't these kittens gorgeous!

This cookie is delicious!

a _____

b _____

c _____

Challenge

Underline the words that mean *said* in these sentences.

1 "I don't want to!" howled Trevor.

2 "Why not?" Jamila whined.

Brain Teaser

Write the speech marks in the correct place.

1 What's the time, Dad? asked Julia.

2 I really like dogs, said Marie.

3 Yuck! squealed John.

Questions and exclamations

A sentence can end with a **full stop**, a **question mark** or an **exclamation mark**.

. ? !

A full stop shows that the sentence is complete.

My tea is ready.

A question mark is used at the end of a sentence to show that a question is being asked.

Is tea ready yet?

An exclamation mark is used at the end of a sentence to show when something is said with a lot of expression or feeling.

"My tea was brilliant!"

Exercise 1

Complete these sentences by adding a full stop, a question mark or an exclamation mark.

a Are we there yet____

b It is raining heavily____

c What was that noise____

d Who is your best friend____

e What do fish eat____

f I love sherbet____

g I hate homework____

h Where is my coat____

i My favourite food is curry____

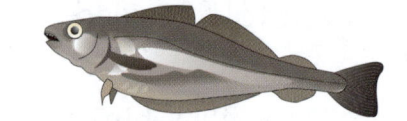

Exercise 2

Complete these sentences by writing in either a full stop or an exclamation mark.

Top Tip: Don't forget to use a capital letter after you have used a full stop. Also, don't use a full stop when you have already used a question mark or an exclamation mark.

a It has rained all week ___

b Don't do that ___

c I like cats ___

d My party was so exciting ___

e It was the scariest film I had ever seen ___

f Bats are nocturnal animals ___

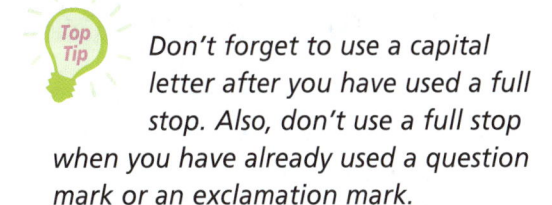

Exercise 3

Now complete these sentences by writing in a full stop, a question mark or an exclamation mark.

a It was the most amazing thing I have ever seen ___

b Sherbet lemons are my favourite sweets ___

c What's your name ___

d How can I help you ___

e Wow ___

Challenge

Add an exclamation mark or a question mark to each of these sentences.

1 Is it time to go now

2 What's that awful smell

3 That was so loud, I jumped out of my skin

Brain Teaser

Write some sentences of your own that finish with either a full stop, a question mark or an exclamation mark.

1 _____

2 _____

3 _____

Understanding text

> When you read, it is important that you **understand** what you are reading. This is called **comprehension**. When you do a comprehension exercise at school, you read a passage and then answer questions to show you have understood what you have read.

Exercise 1

Read this passage. Then have a go at Exercise 2 and Exercise 3.

A great warrior is asked by his pregnant wife for the liver of a Nyamatsane – she craves it. She begs him, saying he must prove he loves her – and that he is the greatest warrior – by hunting a Nyamatsane. He warns that great evil will come of this deed, but the next day he takes his assegai and begins his search. For many long, hot, lonely days he searches – and all at once finds the Nyamatsane dwellings. An old Nyamatsane has been left alone, and he slaughters and skins it, placing its liver in a hide bag. He hears the creatures returning and hides under the skin. They sniff and search, smelling a strange man smell, but are unable to find him. He pretends to eat pebbles, like the creatures, hiding them all the while in his bag.

The hunter creeps away when they curl up to sleep. When the Nyamatsanes find the skin he left behind, they chase with bloodcurdling whoops and cries. The hunter throws down a sparkling pebble from his bag that turns into a glass tower – with him on top! Loyal hunting dogs chase the Nyamatsanes away and the hunter returns to his village.

The wife eats the liver, but then develops a burning thirst. She drinks until no water is left in the village. She ran down to the pounding river – and drank it dry! That night, the animals came out into the cool night air and found the water had gone. A gasping fish tells them what happened. In a rage, they thunder into the village and devour the hunter and his wife – and justice is done.

Exercise 2

Now answer these questions.

a What does the warrior's wife ask him for?

_____

b Which words let us know that the hunter searches for a long time? Copy them out here:

_____

c What does the warrior do to the old Nyamatsane?

_____

Exercise 3

At the end of the story, it says *and justice is done*. Do you think the ending is fair? Explain your answer.

_____

_____

_____

_____

_____

_____

Top Tip: When you are answering a comprehension, write in full sentences. Read the passage once. Then read the questions and skim the passage again looking for words that might help you to answer.

Challenge

Make up a comprehension test for a friend or family member, using your favourite story.

Brain Teaser

1 Who tells the animals what has happened?

_____

2 Why do you think the animals were angry?

_____

_____

UNDERSTANDING TEXT

Synonyms for said

"Hello," said Sam. "Hello," said Mel. "What shall we do today?" said Sam. "I don't know," said Mel.

Gets a bit boring when you repeat the same word – *said* – over and over again, doesn't it?

To make dialogue (when people are talking) more interesting, we can use **synonyms** for the word *said*. Synonyms are different words that mean the same thing.

All these words can be used instead of *said*:
roared whispered
shouted bellowed
uttered replied
muttered explained

Exercise 1

Underline all of the words that mean *said* in the paragraph below.

"What's that?" whispered Fay. "I don't know – but I don't like it!" squealed Ellie. "Perhaps it's a burglar!" hissed Fay. "Cleo!" shrieked Ellie, as a little tortoiseshell cat ran into the room. "Mieow?" the cat replied. "We thought you were an intruder!" laughed Fay.

Exercise 2

Use the words in the box below to complete the sentences. Think about which words meaning *said* fit best with the meaning of the sentences.

> cheered   mumbled   exclaimed   shrieked   sighed

a   "Where is the bathroom?" _____ Susie quietly.

b   "Hurray! Goal!" _____ Alex as his team scored.

c   "Ooh, it's gorgeous!" _____ Katie. "I'm really envious!"

d   "Sorry," _____ Peter. "I didn't mean it."

e   "Yuck! A spider!" _____ Dave.

Top Tip: *Make sure you know how full stops, capital letters and speech marks work when you are using dialogue! Look at the Glossary on pages 100–101 to help you.*

Exercise 3

Now choose four sentences from Exercise 2, but this time use your own words to fill in the gaps. Think of the sense of the sentence before you choose.

a _____

b _____

c _____

d _____

Challenge

Choose a *said* word to complete these sentences:

1   "It's a rat," _____ Julie.

2   "Are we nearly there yet?" _____ Sophie.

3   "If we're quiet, they might not see us!" _____ Helen.

Brain Teaser

Find a better word to replace *said* in these sentences.

1 "It's hot!" said Ben.
_____

2 "Brrr! I'm really cold," said Anna.
_____

3 "A snake!" said Jane.
_____

Active and passive verbs

Remember, **verbs** are words that describe actions.

> The bird is flying.

Flying is the verb, because it tells us about what the bird is doing.

> The cat chased the bird.

Chased is the verb, because it tells us what the cat did.

Verbs can be active or passive.

> The cat walked across the garden.

An active verb tells you what is being done by someone or something.

> The girl was kissed by her granny.

A passive verb tells you about the person or thing the action is being done to.

Verbs change to show us what tense – past, present or future – is being used.

I am looking is the present tense. It is happening now.

I looked is the past tense. It has already happened.

I will look is the future tense. It hasn't happened yet.

Exercise 1

Underline the verbs in these sentences.

a   The fly buzzed past my face.

b   The boy is running along the road.

c   The cat was stroked.

d   The baby is crying.

e   Some dogs were barking.

f   A group of bats flapped through the trees.

Exercise 2

Look at these sentences. Write A if you think the verbs are active and P if you think they are passive.

a _____ The fish was caught.
b _____ The horse neighed.
c _____ Worms wriggle on the ground.
d _____ The windows were cleaned.
e _____ The baby was cuddled.
f _____ The boy laughed.

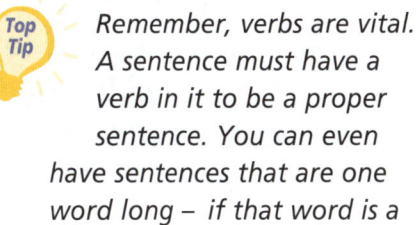

Top Tip: Remember, verbs are vital. A sentence must have a verb in it to be a proper sentence. You can even have sentences that are one word long – if that word is a verb.

Help! Go! Stop!

Exercise 3

Write down which verb tense is being used in these sentences.

a The sun shone yesterday. _____
b The girl will sing later. _____
c I am dancing. _____
d The hamster hid in its bedding. _____
e The tomato will get squashed. _____
f Everyone is watching. _____

Challenge

Can you tell whether verbs are active or passive? Underline the active verbs in these sentences.

1 The girl laughed.
2 The door was closed gently.
3 The sun shone brightly.

Brain Teaser

Read the passage below and underline all of the verbs.

I walked down the road, looking around for my dog. He had run off, barking wildly. As I climbed over a wall to look for him, I fell over. Suddenly, he appeared and jumped on top of me.

Reports and conjunctions

CREATING AND SHAPING TEXTS

Reports about things that have happened need to tell the reader what happened and in what order. They must be accurate and the words you use should keep it interesting for the reader.

Reports use words called **conjunctions** to join sentences, linking them together. These give the reader a sense of the order things happen in.

Conjunctions may be used to:

add to an idea

summarise ideas

explain or illustrate a point

arrange ideas in order

make comparisons and contrasts

Conjunctions include words such as:

and, then, next, eventually, finally, yet, because, so, however

Exercise 1

Imagine you are a reporter for the school newspaper. You have to write a report about sports day. You have written your notes, but they have been mixed up. Put them in the correct order, using the boxes to number the sections.

a   After break, the children came out onto the field.

b   By morning break the parents started to fill the seats on the field.

c   The children lined up for the first race – the egg and spoon!

d   Sports day dawned bright and sunny.

e   It was a great day, enjoyed by everybody.

f   It was won by Judith Nelson.

g   Many more exciting races were run before everyone went home.

Exercise 2

Try to make this report more interesting. Use the conjunctions in the box to fill in the gaps. This will tell your readers the order that things happened in.

> then   so   after that   finally

It was a sunny afternoon. Rosie was hot, _____ she bought an ice-cream. _____ she decided to go swimming.

Top Tip: *Remember, then can be useful but it is horribly over-used! "I went to the sweet shop, then I went to the cake shop, then I went to the park and then I went home."*

_____ she felt a bit cooler. On the way home, she bought an ice-lolly. _____, she felt cool and comfortable!

Exercise 3

Now, on a separate piece of paper, write a report of Danny's day using his diary entry. Use the conjunctions in the box to give your readers an idea of the order things happened in.

> first   after that   then   eventually   next   finally

7.30 Got up and had breakfast.
7.45 Got dressed.
8.00 Watched TV.
9.00 Telephoned Beth to see if she wanted to play football in the park.
2.00 Went to the park and bought crisps and lemonade at the café.
4.00 Went home and played computer games.

Challenge

"My school report was awful! My mum said that, until it was better, I would not be allowed out to play." Can you find the conjunction in the last sentence?

Brain Teaser

Think of a conjunction for each of these groups. Write them in the gaps.

1 add to an idea _____

2 explain or illustrate a point _____

3 arrange ideas in order _____

CREATING AND SHAPING TEXTS

Recounts

A **recount** tells us about an event.

A recount is written in the order in which things happened.

A recount is written in the past tense.

> On Saturday night, Jack and his family had a barbecue. They started to get ready at about 3 o'clock. Mum collected wood for a bonfire and Dad made a big salad. Jack and his Dad went to the shops late in the afternoon to buy some burgers and ice-cream. They chose tutti-frutti. They had to hurry to the baker's shop to get some buns because it shut at 5 o'clock. When they got home, Dad lit the barbecue. Mum and Jack lit some candles in the garden and they waited for their friends to arrive.

Exercise 1

Look at the information below. It gives details about a trip to the pantomime. Now use the space to write a recount of this event.

> Cost: family ticket £24.50. Started at 2pm and finished at 4.30pm. One interval. Ice-cream and sweets for sale. Bus home.

_____
_____
_____
_____
_____

Exercise 2

This recount has been written in the present tense by mistake. Write it out again, changing it to the past tense. You may need another sheet of paper for this exercise.

> I am at the aquarium. There are lots of fantastic fish. I like the shark tunnel best. The café has lots of tasty food, like crisps and squashy cakes. I am buying a toy shark to bring home. I am travelling home on the train.

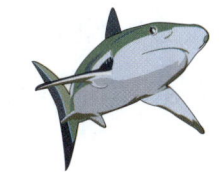

_____
_____
_____
_____

Exercise 3

This recount has been written in the correct tense, but it is jumbled up and not in the correct order. Re-write it on a sheet of paper in the correct order.

a On the way home, we bought some sweets.

b I went to the park.

c "Shall we play football?" she said.

d When I got there I saw my friend Tracey.

e I took a ball with me.

f When we got home, Mum asked Tracey if she'd like to stay to tea.

Top Tip: A recount is in chronological order (the order in which things happened). It is told in the past tense.

Challenge

Write about your day. Fill something in for each time given.

8am _____
9am _____
12 noon _____
1.30pm _____
6pm _____
8pm _____

Brain Teaser

Think of an event you have enjoyed and write a recount of it on a sheet of paper. Do you have a school newspaper or magazine? They may be interested!

CREATING AND SHAPING TEXTS

Writing stories

Do you like reading traditional tales, myths and legends from all over the world? These traditional stories often have common themes, especially where good triumphs over evil!

Traditional tales usually have a beginning like this:

> "A long time ago …"   "There once was …"

The stories are full of heroes and villains. There is often a long journey and there is usually a great problem to solve.

> Have you read *Beauty and the Beast*, *Pinocchio* and *Hansel and Gretel*? What problems had to be solved in these stories?

Exercise 1

You are going to plan your own traditional tale, by adapting one that you already know. You could choose *Cinderella*, *Sleeping Beauty*, *The Three Little Pigs*, or any other traditional tale you know well! You can make up new characters, add new events or even change the way one of the characters acts. If you choose *The Three Billy Goats Gruff*, for example, the troll could be really scared of the goats, who keep teasing him! In the box below plan the outline of your tale.

Top Tip: *Look for myths, legends and traditional tales on the Internet. Try www.nationalgeographic.com/grimm/ for some great versions of 12 traditional tales.*

Exercise 2

Now make notes on a sheet of paper about the characters in your tale. Use the guidelines to help you.

a How many heroes are there?
b Why are they heroes?
c How many villains are there?
d Why are they villains?
e What are the names of your characters?
f What do they look like?
g What kind of things do they say?

Exercise 3

Now write your tale. Write a rough draft first, then, when you're ready, you can write it on a computer or a sheet of paper. If you like, you can add in some illustrations (drawings). When your story is finished, try to learn it by heart. Then tell it to an audience – just like they did in the old days.

Challenge

Write a synopsis – a short description containing the main events – of your favourite traditional tale here:

_____

_____

_____

_____

Brain Teaser

Think about the story of Cinderella. Name the heroes and villains. Then explain the problem that had to be overcome.

Who were your favourite characters? Why?

Letters

Formal letters are the type of thing sent by your school, to tell the adults you live with about reports or meetings. They contain formal language.

Informal letters are the type of chatty letters you send to friends. They contain informal language.

Dear Mrs Nelson,

We take great pleasure inviting you to our prize-giving ceremony. Your son Paul has won a prize for mathematics. We know you will share our pride in this achievement, and look forward to seeing you.

Yours faithfully,

Mr H. Master

Hi Sam!

Guess what? I've won a prize for maths! Amazing, eh? Mum's chuffed, so I'll be in her good books for a bit! Are you coming to stay soon?

Talk to you later,

Paul

Exercise 1

Imagine you have built a fabulous wildlife garden. Write a formal letter below to invite the Prime Minister to your school. Remember to use formal language – no contractions (*isn't*, *can't* and so on). Finish the letter *Yours faithfully*.

_____

_____

_____

_____

_____

Exercise 2

Now write an informal letter telling your auntie that the Prime Minister is coming to visit your school. Remember to use informal language or your auntie might think you are cross with her!

_____
_____
_____
_____
_____
_____
_____
_____
_____
_____

Top Tip: *Look at letters from school and see if you can spot the formal language.*

Exercise 3

Look at the formal and informal letters opposite. Underline the things that tell you whether the letter is formal or informal.

Challenge

When you write to relatives and friends, you can be informal.

Write a letter to a member of your family. Remember to use informal language or they might think that you are cross with them!

Brain Teaser

Formal or informal?

1 Which sort of letter would start *Dear Sir*?
   _____

2 Which sort of letter would end *Love from*?
   _____

3 Which sort of letter would end *Yours faithfully*?
   _____

CREATING AND SHAPING TEXTS

Shape poems

Shape poems are poems that are written in the shape of the thing being written about.

A leaf poem could be written in the shape of a leaf.

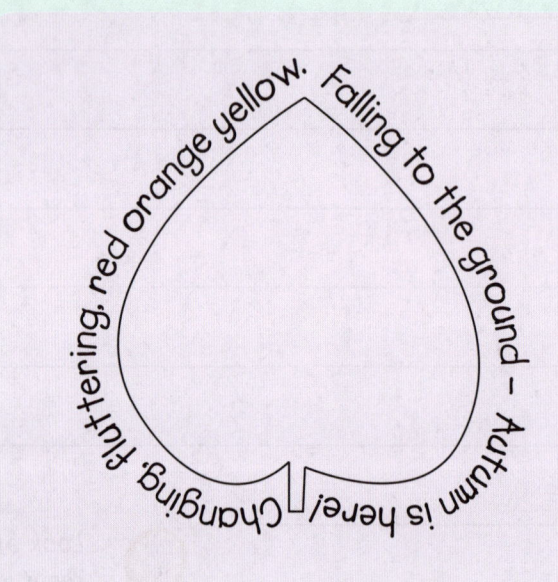

Falling to the ground – Autumn is here! Changing, fluttering, red orange yellow.

Exercise 1

Write a poem about winter. Think of six words to do with snow and cold weather. Then write them below. Some words have already been suggested to get you started.

icicle   sparkle   glittering   frosty

TEXT STRUCTURE AND ORGANISATION

Exercise 2

Now write your poem from Exercise 1 in the shape of a snowman. Use the shape below to guide you.

Top Tip: Look for shape poems on the Internet. Just type 'shape poems' into a search engine and see what pops out!

Exercise 3

Write a shape poem about something you are interested in. It could be snakes, new clothes, football – you choose. Write some words in this box to get you started. Then, on a piece of paper, draw your shape and write in your poem.

Challenge

Can you write a shape poem about a big hairy spider?

Write some words to use in the poem below.

Brain Teaser

Write your poem in the shape of a spider here.

Spellings

The words being tested are:

cooking	chopped	touch
show	pieces	remove
soap	thick	pastry
measure	juicy	tight
began	apple	straight
golden	gently	several
weigh	boil	squares

Ask an adult to read this passage to you while you listen. Then, the adult should read the passage again, this time pausing after each underlined word so you can write down how it is spelled on a separate piece of paper.

Susie was appearing on the children's <u>cooking</u> <u>show</u> *Sticky Fingers*. Her Mum was going to help her. They washed their hands thoroughly with <u>soap</u>, and then started to <u>measure</u> things out carefully. They <u>began</u> with <u>golden</u> sugar. Susie asked her Mum to <u>weigh</u> out some butter, which they then <u>chopped</u> into <u>pieces</u>. They added <u>thick</u>, <u>juicy</u> slices of <u>apple</u> to a pan of water, which they brought <u>gently</u> to the <u>boil</u>.

"Don't <u>touch</u>, Mum! It's hot!" Susie laughed. "Now – we need to <u>remove</u> the cores from these other apples, and pack them into the <u>pastry</u> case, nice and <u>tight</u>. Try to cut <u>straight</u> pieces. Cut <u>several</u> <u>squares</u> to put on the pie as decoration."

Handwriting

Handwriting is assessed as a part of other tests – so it is a good idea to practise!

Copy out the section of a poem shown below on a piece of paper, in your best handwriting. Try to make all of the ascenders (the long sticks on letters such as *d* and *k*) and descenders (the long tails on letters such as *p* and *g*) on the letters an equal size.

That's My Boy!

The whistle shrieks, and we're off!
Charging after the ball
A herd of cartoon hippos
Churning the field to mush.

I break away from the pack
Dodge left, feint right,
Blazing up the field, turbo charged.
With a blast – it's in the net!

I whirl, arms outstretched,
Whooping boys tangle round my neck.
I slip and wriggle downwards
Peering into the boiling crowd.

The joy fossilises in my chest,
Falls, and lodges in my gut
Cold, like the ice pack Sir carries for injuries.
My Dad missed it.

Wait – arms and legs pumping,
Tie flying ludicrously over his shoulder,
A familiar shape is running across the field.
He's shouting something I can't quite hear.

Then his voice booms, and people turn to look.
"Attaboy!" He's shouting. "That's my boy!"

He's here! He's here!

Story writing

Choose one of the story titles below and write a story. Spend 10 to 15 minutes planning the story and 35 minutes writing it. Use the planning sheet to help you. Try to keep your writing neat! You will need spare paper to write your story.

Titles

Lost in the snow

A kitten for Christmas

Space slug!

Drifting

Where is the story set?

Who are the main characters? What are they like?

Is there a problem to solve, or a challenge to face?

An exciting opening:

A good strong ending:

Think of some descriptions to use in your story:

interesting words brainstorm

TEST PRACTICE

Comprehension

Grow your own gems!

You need: sugar, spoon, warm water, cup and saucer, food colouring, thread.

1 Put some warm water in a cup.

2 Add a few drops of food colouring.

3 Stir in some sugar. Keep adding until no more will dissolve in the water.

4 Pour a little of the mixture into a saucer and put it in a warm place – on the radiator or on a sunny window sill. Cover the rest of the mixture and put it somewhere cool.

5 When the water evaporates (disappears into the air), you will be left with some small crystals.

6 Choose the biggest crystal. Then ask an adult to help you tie it onto a piece of thread.

7 Tie the other end of the thread to a spoon. Rest the spoon across the top of the cup of water. The crystal will dangle from the thread, into the water.

8 Leave the cup somewhere warm and the crystal will keep growing!

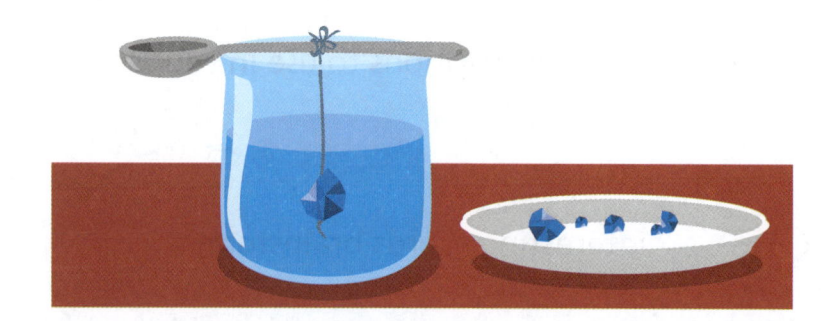

1   What do you need in order to grow your own gems? Make a list. (1 mark)

_____

2   What does the word *evaporate* mean? (1 mark)

_____

3   Why do you have to leave the mixture somewhere warm? (1 mark)

_____

4   What is the spoon used for? (1 mark)

_____

5   Find and make a list of four verbs in the instructions. (2 mark)

_____

_____

6   Draw step-by-step pictures to present the instructions in a different way. You may write captions beneath the pictures, but you should try to give as much information as possible in a visual way – using pictures. (4 mark)

Total
10 marks

Writing letters

TEST PRACTICE

Choose **one** letter to write from the two choices below:

1. A formal letter to complain about bad service in a fast food restaurant. Don't forget to use formal language, and to set your address out properly!

2. An informal letter telling a friend about a great party. Remember, you should use informal language!

Glossary

adjective Describing word, used to make sentences more interesting. The fluffy (adjective) cat (noun) purred

apostrophe ' Shows that a letter or letters are missing from words. *Is not* becomes *isn't* (the apostrophe replaces the o). *She has* becomes *she's* (the apostrophe replaces the ha). See contractions. It is also used as the possessive, such as *the cat's tail*

brainstorm Jotting down notes at the beginning of a writing task to help you to get organised.

capital letter Upper case letter. For example, ABC is used for names and places

comma , A punctuation mark. It shows where you need to pause in a sentence

comprehension understanding what a text is about

conjunction a word used to link sentences or clauses, or to correct words within a phrase

contractions Shortened versions of words with letters left out shown by an apostrophe: couldn't, wouldn't, isn't

exclamation mark ! A punctuation mark. It shows feeling, like surprise or shock

fiction Stories that have been made up

full stop . A punctuation mark. It tells you when a sentence has ended

homonyms Words that have the same spelling but different meanings, for example, pick can mean: choose carefully, a tool, detach (pick fruit)

homophones Words that have different spellings but sound alike – for example: bear/bare, pair/pear, grate/great

lower case Letters that are not capitals, for example, abc

non-fiction Reports, recipes and instructions. They tell us facts. They are not made up like fiction

noun The naming word – a thing, person or place. Book (thing), Lynn (person), Durham (place)

plural Describing more than one. The cats' tails

prefix The letters that you put before a word that already exists to change its meaning. For example, the prefix pre is used before the word paid (prepaid) to mean paid in advance

pronoun A word to replace a noun. It can also refer back to a noun. The most common pronouns are: I, you, he, she, it, we and they

punctuation The marks that divide words up into phrases and sentences – for example, full stop . comma , exclamation ! question mark ?

question mark ? A punctuation mark. It tells you that a question is being asked

recount a report that describes events in chronological order, or the order in which they happened

singular Describing one thing. A cat is singular. Some cats is plural

speech marks " " punctuation marks that surround direct speech. Other punctuation goes inside them, e.g. "Goodbye," said Mum

suffix The letters that you can put at the end of an existing word, such as *ly*. Suffixes can often change nouns to adjectives

syllables Chunks of sound in a word. Alligator has four: al/li/ga/tor

synonym A word that means almost the same as another word, for example, shut, slam, close. Synonyms make your writing much more interesting

upper case Upper case letters are capitals, for example, ABC

verb Action (or doing) words such as: talking, washing, playing

Notes

Notes

Notes

LEARN AND PRACTISE — Maths and English Age 7–8 — Answers

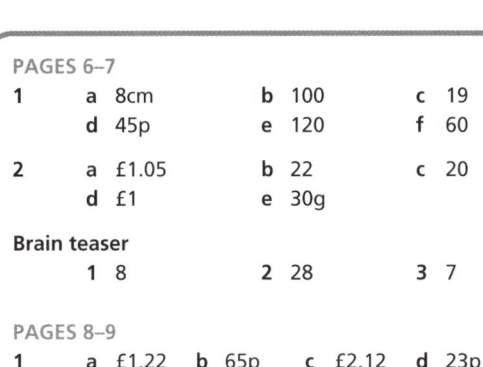

PAGES 6–7

1. a 8cm b 100 c 19 d 45p e 120 f 60
2. a £1.05 b 22 c 20 d £1 e 30g

Brain teaser
1. 8   2. 28   3. 7

PAGES 8–9

1. a £1.22 b 65p c £2.12 d 23p
2. a 70p b £1.10 c 95p d 25p e £1.60 f £1.25
3. a £1.64
   b £13.65
   c £1.25
   d 75p
   e (20p, 10p, 50p, 2p coins in wallet)

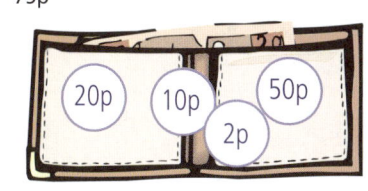

Brain teaser
1. £1, 20p, 10p, 5p, 1p coins
2. £2, 50p, 10p, 5p, 2p coins
3. 50p, 20p, 20p, 2p, 2p coins
4. £2, £1, 10p, 2p, 1p coins

PAGES 10–11

1. a 35 37 39   d 512 612 712
   b 72 70 68   e 56 46 36
   c 82 92 102 f 128 118 108
2. a 21 25 33   b 25 13 10
   c 16 31 36   d 50 34 30
3. a 137 *138* 139 *140* 141 *142*
   b *240* 239 238 237 *236* 235
   c 809 *810* 811 *812* 813 *814* 815 *816*

Brain teaser
1. -4 -3 -2 -1 0 1 2
2. -3 -2 -1 0 1 2 3

PAGES 12–13

1. six hundred and ninety-four — 694
   three hundred and sixty-eight — 368
   six hundred and eighty — 680
   nine hundred and sixty-four — 964
   one hundred and twenty-four — 124
   six hundred and eighty-three — 683

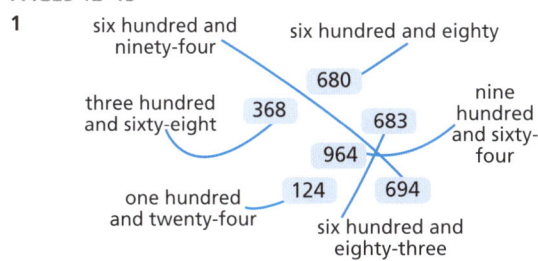

2. a 90 d 700 + 30 + 4
   b 500 + 30 + 8 e 800 + 40 + 9
   c 700 + 40 + 6 f 200 + 90 + 3

3. a 680 420 810 900
   b 32 40 74 68

Brain teaser
1. 20 90   2. 30 60

PAGES 14–15

1. a 242 b 606 c 592 d 796
2. a Any number between 384 and 399. Any number between 399 and 406.
   b Any number smaller than 615. Any number between 615 and 637.
   c Any two numbers between 825 and 878, the first smaller than the second.
3. a 284ml 480ml 714ml 738ml 842ml
   b 560g 650g 681g 856g 865g
4. 381 337 314 373 356 on number line 300–400

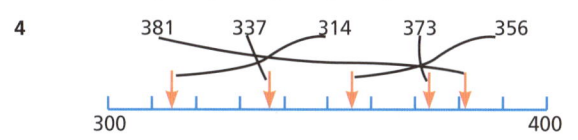

Brain teaser
1. 219 216   2. 370 374
3. 684 681

PAGES 16–17

1. a 50 b 80 c 10 d 80 e 60 f 50 g 60 h 60 i 40
2. a 300 b 200 c 200 d 300 e 700 f 600 g 500 h 900 i 200
3. 27→30, 42→40, 58→60, 74→70, 85→90, 96→100
4. Any numbers between 350 and 449.

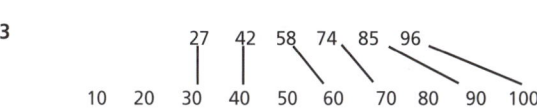

Brain teaser
1. 1400   2. 3100   3. 6200

PAGES 18-19

1. a $\frac{1}{2}$ b $\frac{1}{3}$ c $\frac{1}{5}$ d $\frac{1}{4}$
2. (shaded shapes)
3. a 3 b 3 c 4
4. Any 5 parts coloured red. Any 10 parts coloured blue.

Brain teaser
1. $\frac{1}{2}$ 2. $\frac{3}{4}$ 3. $\frac{1}{3}$
4. $\frac{9}{10}$ 5. $\frac{3}{10}$ 6. $\frac{5}{9}$

MATHS

PAGES 20–21

1 a

	4	6	2
7	11	13	9
3	7	9	5
8	12	14	10

b

+	6	3	11
5	11	8	16
9	15	12	20
4	10	7	15

c

	6	4	5
12	18	16	17
14	20	18	19
9	15	13	14

2 a 5 **b** 3 **c** 3
  d 7 **e** 7 **f** 6

3

a	b	c	d
9	13	3	9
8	15	2	8
10	11	5	8
10	13	7	6
7	13	4	9
7	11	4	7
9	16	5	4
9	15	1	9

Brain teaser

1 7 + 4 + 3 = 14
2 9 − 2 + 8 = 15
3 6 + 3 − 4 = 5
4 8 − 2 − 4 = 2
5 11 + 6 − 3 = 14

PAGES 22-23

1 a 2 × 9, 9 × 2, 3 × 6, 6 × 3 = 18
  b 5 × 4, 4 × 5, 2 × 10, 10 × 2 = 20
  c 6 × 4, 4 × 6, 12 × 2, 2 × 12 = 24

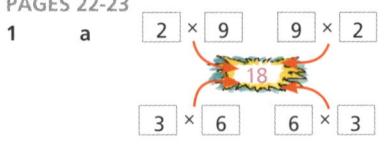

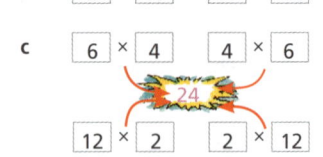

2
  a 7 × 2 = 14; 4 × 4 = 16; 5 × 9 = 45; 3 × 8 = 24; 6 × 6 = 36; 4 × 3 = 12
  b 8 × 3 = 24; 9 × 2 = 18; 5 × 5 = 25; 6 × 7 = 42; 10 × 4 = 40; 4 × 9 = 36
  c 7 × 9 = 63; 5 × 8 = 40; 6 × 3 = 18; 4 × 7 = 28; 9 × 8 = 72; 5 × 6 = 30

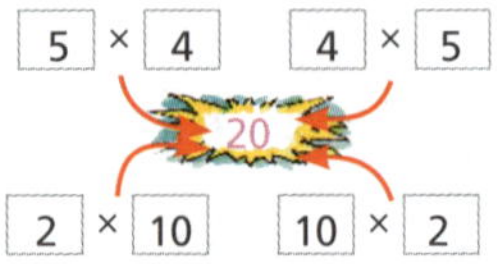

3 a IN → ×3 → OUT

IN	4	5	10	7	3
OUT	12	15	30	21	9

b IN → ×4 → OUT

IN	2	8	7	4	5
OUT	8	32	28	16	20

Brain teaser

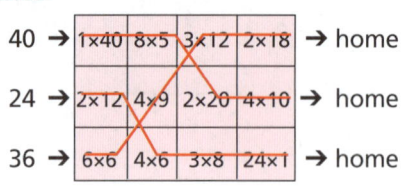

40 → 1×40, 8×5, 3×12, 2×18 → home
24 → 2×12, 4×9, 2×20, 4×10 → home
36 → 6×6, 4×6, 3×8, 24×1 → home

PAGES 24–25

1 a 70, 76   **d** 120, 124   **g** 110, 117
  b 110, 115 **e** 90, 96   **h** 110, 111
  c 90, 105   **f** 130, 144 **i** 130, 139

2

19	24	43
32	18	50
51	42	93

21	34	55
26	17	43
47	51	98

15	31	46
24	29	53
39	60	99

3 72+45=117... pairs shown: 72, 45, 82, 18, 27, 63, 73, 37, 65, 28, 55, 35

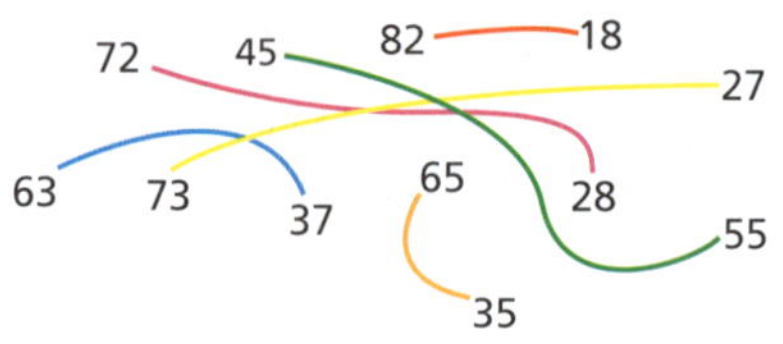

Brain teaser

1 29 and 26   2 44
3 72   4 29, 43 and 18

PAGE 26–27

1 a 19 **b** 13 **c** 25
  d 25 **e** 27

2 a 38 − 7 − 45; 13 − 16; 51 − 22 − 29
  b 54 − 26 − 28; 18 − 9; 36 − 17 − 19

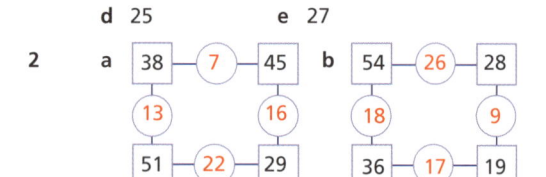

3 a 15 **b** 39 **c** 40 **d** 60
  e 64 **f** 27 **g** 140 **h** 48

Brain teaser

1 32 and 25   2 22
3 25   4 false

PAGES 28–29

1 a 95   **b** 182 **c** 93   **d** 331
  e 135 **f** 180 **g** 174 **h** 510

2 a 26   **b** 105 **c** 242
  d 55   **e** 132 **f** 68

3

```
  [5] 7        [3] 6 5       [1] 3 [0]
+   3 8      +   [5] 9      -   8 6
─────────    ─────────      ─────────
    9 [5]        4 2 4            4 4
```

```
  1 [6] 4      1 [9] 7
+   4 [3]    -   5 3
─────────    ─────────
    2 0 7      1 4 4
```

Brain teaser

```
  1 8 [3]      2 1 6        2 9 [7]
+   4 7      -   5 [4]     +   [5] 4
─────────    ─────────     ─────────
  [2] 3 0      [1] [6] 2     3 5 1
```

PAGES 30–31

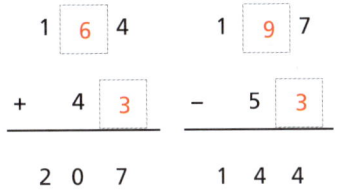

1 a 6   b 5   c 7
   d 3   e 6   f 3
2 a 2 r 2 b 7 r 1 c 7 r 1
   d 5 r 4 e 4 r 3 f 10 r 2
3 a 6   b 6   c 9   d 4

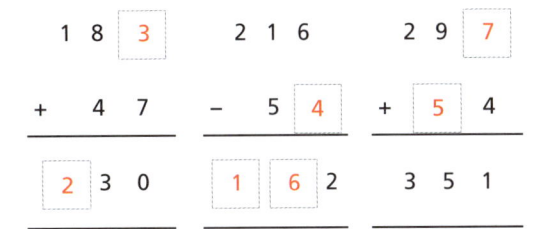

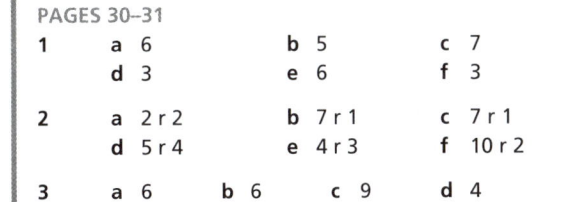

Brain teaser

2 groups of 15
15 groups of 2
3 groups of 10
10 groups of 3
5 groups of 6
6 groups of 5

PAGES 32–33

1 [quadrilateral / not a quadrilateral sorting]

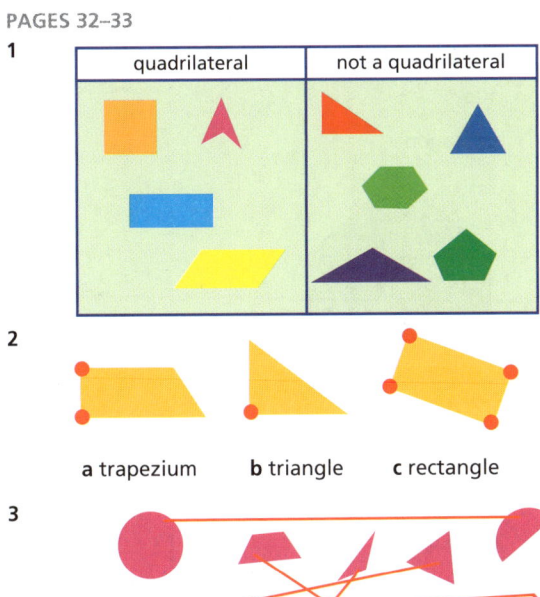

2 a trapezium   b triangle   c rectangle

3 [shapes matched with lines]

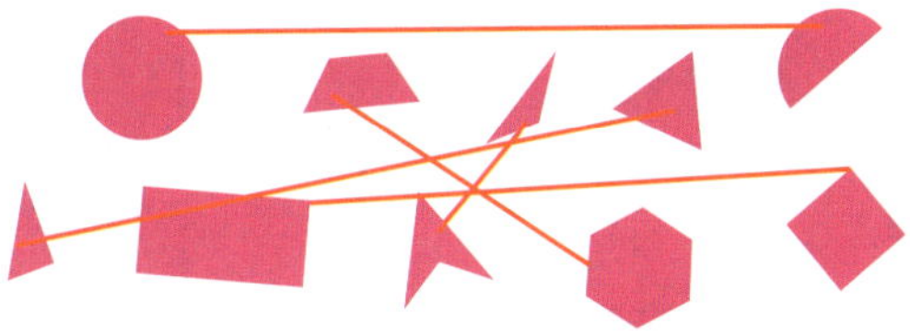

Brain teaser

There are 30 triangles.

PAGES 34–35

1 a cuboids 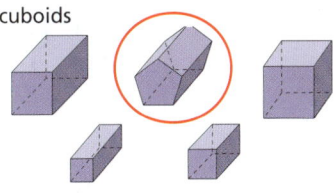
   b pyramids 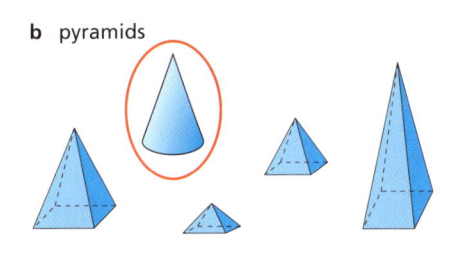
   c cylinders 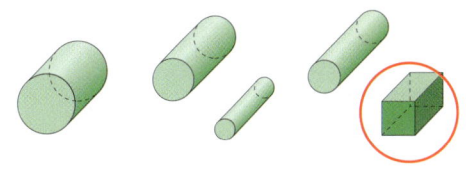
   d cones

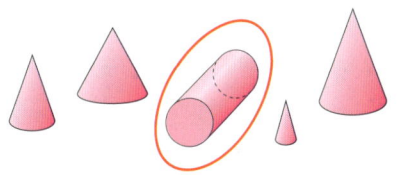

2 a False   b False   c True
   d False   e True

3 Venn diagram — 3D-shapes: prisms {a, e}, intersection {g}, some triangle faces {b, d}; outside {c, f}

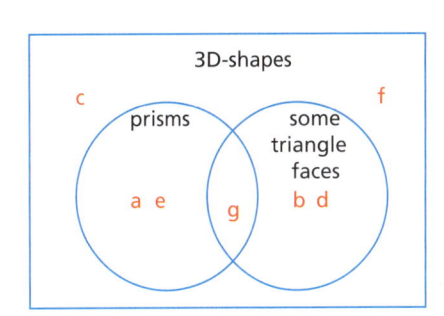

Brain Teaser

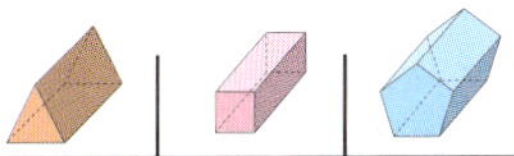

faces	5	6	7
edges	9	12	15
vertices	6	8	10

PAGES 36–37

1 a, b, c, d, e, f, g, h [lines of symmetry shown on shapes]

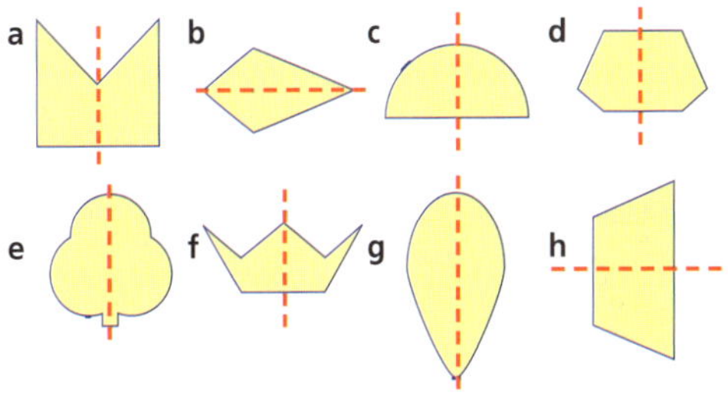

2 a [tree with line of symmetry]   b [butterfly with line of symmetry]

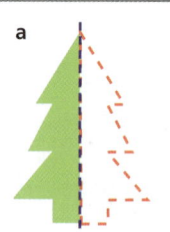

3 a [H with lines of symmetry]   b [rectangle with lines of symmetry]   c [oval with lines of symmetry]

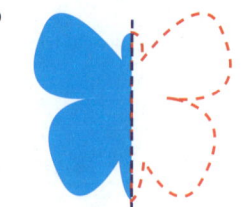

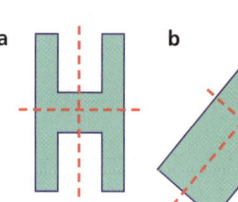

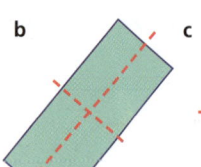

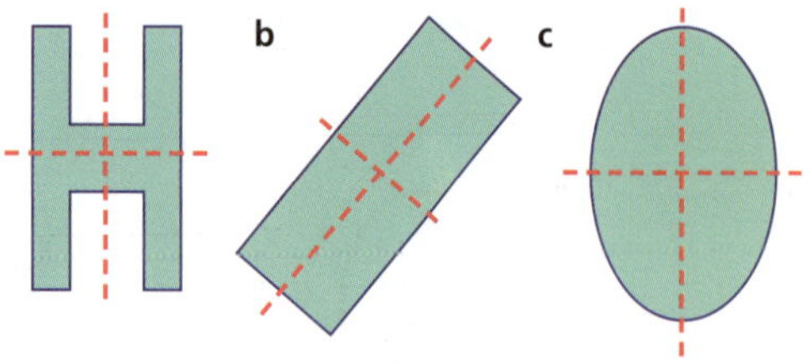

Brain teaser

4 [square with line of symmetry]

PAGES 38–39

1 a East   d North   g South
   b South e North   h North
   c West   f West   i North

2 a Bay 1   b Bay 4   c Bay 2   d Bay 3

Brain teaser

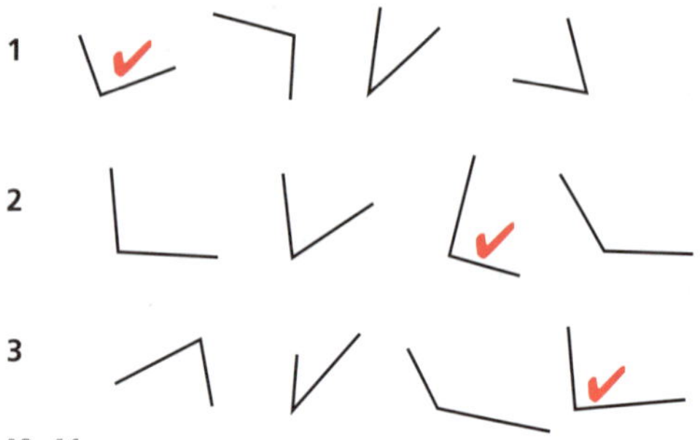

1 [right angle ticked]
2 [right angle ticked]
3 [right angle ticked]

PAGES 40–41

1 a 4cm   b 6.5cm   c 4.9cm
   d 7.6cm e 3.3cm   f 6cm

2 a 300ml b 450ml   c 350ml
   d 150ml e 200ml

Brain teaser

Perimeter = 14cm

PAGES 42–43

1 a 3.10   b 7.30   c 6.40   d 11.15
   e 1.55   f 4.45   g 12.05 h 9.20

2 a 15 minutes   b 120 minutes
   c 30 seconds   d August

3 a 7.45   b 10.25   c 2.50   d 12.35
   [four clocks]

Brain teaser

The actual time for all the clocks is 3.55 [clock]

PAGES 44–45

1 a 55   b Javed   c 45
   d 85   e 25

2 a 40
   b 2.40pm
   c 10
   d Any answer between 2 and 19.
   e Any estimate between 123 and 147.

Brain teaser

house number	black cat	ginger cat	white cat
1	Sam		
2			Jack
3		Ruth	

Test Practice

PAGES 46–51

1   9
2   Four hundred and one
3   4.45
4   6.15
5   pyramid (rectangular based)
6   45p
7   44
8   29
9   150cm
10 65 (reading across the rows:
    25 + 40 = 65, 30 + 65 = 95, 35 + 40 = 75)
11 [semicircle with line of symmetry]
12 81
13 458
14 485
15 3.5kg
16 10p
17 pentagon
18 [pentagon with two vertices marked]
19 12
20 24
21 250ml
22 a and b
23 600
24 17
25 18, 21 and 27

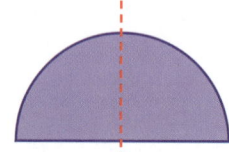

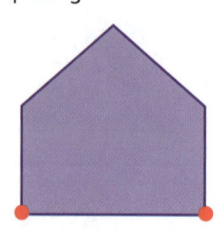

PAGES 54–55

1. The answers which should be circled are: b, c and f.
2. Answers will vary, but should include useful clue words and what the objects might be.

Brain teaser
Answers will vary, but children should listen to a partner talk about school uniform or homework, before giving their own opinion.

PAGES 56–57

1.
   a un
   b re
   c mis
   d non
   e anti
   f pre
   g ex
   h pre
   i in
   j non

2.
   a non
   b mis
   c non
   d mis
   e non
   f non
   g non
   h mis

3.
   a pre
   b in
   c mis
   d non
   e anti
   f un

Brain teaser
1 mis
2 non
3 in
4 un
5 mis

PAGES 58–59

1.
   a hide
   b ball
   c gum
   d ball
   e hide
   f gum

2.
   a I'll
   b allowed
   c altar
   d eight
   e eye
   f ball

3.
   a ewe
   c heel
   b flea
   d groan

Brain teaser
1 sees
2 side
3 their
4 to

PAGES 60–61

1.
   a mustn't
   b can't
   c isn't
   d shouldn't
   e hasn't
   f you're
   g I've
   h he's
   i haven't

2.
   a will not
   b cannot
   c she is
   d he will
   e we have
   f they will
   g has not
   h you are

3. Passage should be rewritten with the following alterations: do not, It is, has not, there is.

Brain teaser
1 I've
2 we'll
3 shouldn't
4 isn't

PAGES 62–63

1.
   a + ly = kindly
   b + ful = playful
   c + ic = heroic
   d + able = loveable
   e + worthy = blameworthy

2.
   a ish
   b ish
   c ful
   d ful
   e ful
   f ful
   g ful
   h ish
   i ish
   j ful

3. a, b, c, e, g, h

Brain teaser
These words should be crossed out:
1 trustish
2 wishworthy
3 penniable

PAGES 64–65

1. Spellings should be learned using the look/say/cover/write/check method.
2. Spellings should be learned.
3. Possible answers include:
   a fat, cat, hat
   b hall, fall, call
   c hut, put, but
   d bad, sad, mad
   e pig, fig, dig
   f fin, tin, win
   g bake, lake, take

Brain teaser
1 did, hid, kid, lid, rid
2 fit, hit, kit, lit, nit, pit, sit, wit
3 face, lace, pace

PAGES 66–67

1. Answers should include two of the following:
   a son, less, on
   b dance, bun, an
   c story, his, is
   d hell, she, he
   e we, the, at, eat, her
   f change, hang, an

2. Answers should include three of the following:
   a an, tan, admit, it
   b city, electric, it, elect
   c must, tar, star
   d price, rice, ice
   e did, lend, end
   f and, stand, an, tan

3.
   a not, an, other, her
   b arch, chive, hive, arc
   c bull, tin, let, in, bullet
   d air, plane, lane, an

Brain teaser
cart, ridge, art, rid, car

PAGES 68–69

1.
   a racing
   b fluttering
   c squeaking
   d singing
   e walked
   f shining

2.
   a smile
   b walk
   c laugh
   d frown
   e eat
   f dance

3. Possible answers include:
   a chased
   b spat, growled
   c climb, scamper
   d twinkle, shine
   e laughing, giggling
   f slithered

Brain teaser
1. gobble 2. observe
3. yell, scream

PAGES 70–71
1. a slimy
   b shiny, red
   c enormous, grey, wrinkly
   d smelly
   e big, bad, ugly
   f sparkling, glittered
   g tabby
2. a scalding   d hilarious
   b enormous   e freezing, icy
   c miniscule
3. Possible answers include:
   a ferocious   e brilliant
   b massive   f terrifying
   c freezing   g scalding
   d gorgeous

Brain teaser
1. huge   2. ferocious
3. gigantic   4. scalding

PAGES 72–73
1. a it   d us
   b she   e they
   c he   f me
2. a she   d My, They
   b them   e I, It
   c he, it
3. a David and Tina   b horses
   c Ellie

Brain teaser
1. I   2. We
3. They

PAGES 74–75
1. a It's time for school!
   b We are going to the shops
   c Would you like to come to my party?
   d I don't like sprouts. I want an ice-cream!
   e Can you help me to open this jar?
   f Would you like to borrow this book?

   Because they have speech marks around them.
2. a "Put on your wellies, Jo!" called mum.
   b "Every time we go to the swimming baths," said Harvey, "I get really cold."
   c "Stop that!" shouted the teacher.
   d "You are such a good footballer!" sighed the girl.
3. Possible sentences include:
   a "Stop! Don't run in school!" said the teacher.
   b "Ahh! Aren't these kittens gorgeous!" sighed Emma.
   c "This cookie is delicious," munched Peter.

Brain teaser
1. "What's the time, Dad?" asked Julia.
2. "I really like dogs," said Marie.
3. "Yuck!" squealed John.

PAGES 76–77
1. a ?   f !
   b .   g !
   c ?   h ?
   d ?   i .
   e ?
2. a .   d !
   b !   e !
   c .   f .
3. a !   d ?
   b .   e !
   c ?

Brain teaser
Possible answers include:
1. How old are you?
2. I'm called Elizabeth.
3. Look out!

PAGES 78–79
1. Passage should be read carefully.
2. a the liver of a Nyamatsane
   b many, long, hot, lonely days
   c slaughters and skins it
3. Answer can be yes or no, as long as the answer is justified.

Brain teaser
1. a gasping fish
2. Because the woman was greedy and drank all of the water, so there was no water for the animals.

PAGES 80–81
1. whispered, squealed, hissed, shrieked, replied, laughed
2. a mumbled   d exclaimed
   b cheered   e shrieked
   c sighed
3. Answers will vary.

Brain teaser
Possible answers include:
1. moaned   2. shivered
3. screamed

PAGES 82–83
1. a buzzed   d crying
   b running   e barking
   c stroked   f flapped
2. a P   d P
   b A   e P
   c A   f A
3. a past   d past/present
   b future   e future
   c present   f present

Brain teaser
walked, looking, run, barking, climbed, look, fell, appeared, jumped

PAGES 84–85
1. a 3   e 7
   b 2   f 5
   c 4   g 6
   d 1
2. so, Then, After that, Finally

3 First, Danny got up and had breakfast. Then he got dressed. After that he watched TV. Next he telephoned Beth to see if she wanted to play football. Then they went to the park. Eventually they bought crisps and lemonade at the café. Finally they went home and played computer games.

Brain teaser

Possible answers include:
1 also   2 because
3 after that

PAGES 86–87

1 Possible answers include:
We went to the 2pm pantomime and it cost £24.50. There was one interval when we bought ice-cream and sweets. The panto finished at 4.30pm. After that we got the bus home.

2 I was at the aquarium. There were lots of fantastic fish. I liked the shark tunnel best. The café had lots of tasty food, like crisps and squashy cakes. I bought a toy shark to bring home. I travelled home on the train.

3 The correct order is: b, e, d, c, a, f.

Brain teaser

A recount in the past tense, in chronological order, of an event.

PAGES 88–89

1 An example of planning if, for example, The Three Little Pigs was chosen (could be done with different story) would be:
  a the three pigs
  b at the three pigs' houses
  c the heroes = pigs;
     villain = wolf
  d the wolf dresses up as a pig and manages to get into the pigs' houses
  e The pigs get the wolf to help them make a pie (the pigs realise that the new pig is actually the wolf) and the pigs push the wolf into the pie. They cook it and have wolf pie.

2 There are many answers to all questions. Examples for the adapted Three Little Pigs tale are:
  a three
  b Because they're clever (depending on the tale used).
  c one, the wolf
  d Because he plans to kill the pigs.
  e James, Andrew, Alex (pigs)
     The wolf is called William.
  f James, Andrew and Alex are little pink pigs. William is grey and has large, fanged teeth.
  g Wolf: "I am going to eat you whole." Pigs: "Not if we have anything to do about it."

3 Child should write a story containing the elements discussed in the previous questions.

Brain teaser

A variety of answers such as: The heroes are Cinderella, the prince, the fairy godmother and the animals that get turned into the coachmen. The villains are the evil stepmother and the ugly step-sisters. The problem is that the stepmother and step-sisters are cruel to Cinderella and will not let her go to the Ball.

PAGES 90–91

1 A letter using formal language, with no contractions, no slang, and finished with "Yours faithfully".

2 A letter using informal language, which can include "chatty" language and slang, and may finish with "love".

3 Dear Mrs Nelson,

We take great pleasure inviting you to our prize-giving ceremony. Your son Paul has won a prize for mathematics. We know you will share our pride in this achievement, and look forward to seeing you.

Yours faithfully,

Mr H. Master

Hi Sam!

Guess what? I've won a prize for maths! Amazing, eh? Mum's chuffed, so I'll be in her good books for a bit! Are you coming to stay soon?

Talk to you later,

Paul

Brain teaser

1 a formal letter
2 an informal letter
3 a formal letter

PAGES 92–93

1 Possible answers include: blizzard, white, blanketed, hushed, snowman, toboggan.

2 A diagram of a snowman with a poem inside.

3 Many answers are possible, such as the shape of a snake with a snake poem inside, or a football with a football poem inside.

Brain teaser

A diagram of a spider with a poem inside.

TEST PRACTICE

PAGE 94

Spellings

Learn the spellings! Use look/say/cover/write/check, as an aid.

PAGE 95

Handwriting

The handwriting exercise should be neat with all of the letters clearly identifiable.

PAGES 96–97

Story writing

Plan the story using the techniques discussed. This must include a strong beginning and end. Careful thought and consideration of the character's appearance, attitude and what the villains / heroes are like. Where is the story set? What problem does the hero have to overcome and how does the hero overcome the problem?

PAGES 98–99
Comprehension
1. You need sugar, a spoon, warm water, a cup and saucer, food colouring and a thread.
2. *Evaporate* refers to when water seems to disappear into the air.
3. You leave it somewhere warm so the crystals carry on growing.
4. The spoon is to tie to the thread so that the crystal will dangle into the water.
5. Four verbs are: growing, tie, leave, pour.
6. Diagram of pictures showing the instructions.

PAGE 100
Writing letters
1. Remember to include formal language, and what is wrong with the service.
2. Use informal language. It could start with "Hi" and finish with "Love from".

Letts Educational, an imprint of HarperCollins*Publishers*
77–85 Fulham Palace Road
London W6 8JB

Telephone: 0844 576 8126
Fax: 0844 576 8131
Email: education@harpercollins.co.uk
Website: www.lettsrevision.com

ISBN 9781844196937

Text© Paul Broadbent and Lynn Huggins-Cooper

Design and illustration © 2008 Letts Educational, an imprint of HarperCollins*Publishers*

This edition first published in 2012

Every effort has been made to trace copyright holders and obtain their permission for the use of copyright material. The authors and publishers will gladly receive information enabling them to rectify any error or omission in subsequent editions. All facts are correct at time of going to press.

All our Rights Reserved. No part of the publication may be produced, stored in a retrieval system, or transmitted, in any form or by any means, electronic, mechanical, photocopying, recording or otherwise, without the prior permission of Letts Educational.